"LANSDALE'S GENIUS LIES in tilling the soil of human potential. *Cultivating Inspired Leaders* gives us wisdom as well as practical skills for our everyday lives. The volume's humanist philosophy empowers the reader to embrace attitudes and commitments essential to improving the human condition. Most importantly, Lansdale teaches us how a good sense of humor can reveal universal truths even amidst a fragmenting and multicultural world."

Philip O. Geier, Ph.D.
President, United World College

"BRUCE LANSDALE himself epitomizes the qualities of the Leader-Manager that he describes in this book. He has lived by these clear-cut and commonsense principles, which are too often ignored by those who would do good *to* their fellow creatures rather than *with* them. Members of organizations—profit, non-profit, or governmental—will improve their effectiveness if they ask themselves the questions he poses and take to heart the lessons he offers. Mr. Lansdale's step-by-step guide to management and human relations should inspire readers and prospective "Leaders" to strive for the same benevolent spirit of his work."

C. William Kontos
Vice President, Global Business Access, Ltd.

"I MET BRUCE LANSDALE thirty-seven years ago when he was the Director of the American Farm School in Greece. I had many opportunities to observe the splendid ways in which he prompted and inspired staff and teachers, as well as students, to reach for excellence. Bruce now documents in detail how innovative forms of management can be taught and how to 'cultivate' inspired leaders. He has written a fascinating and entertaining book."

Eve Labouisse
Vice Chairman, Board of Trustees,
The American Farm School

"BRUCE LANSDALE HAS an uncanny way of applying his knowledge, wisdom, and especially his experiences that makes this book worth reading, rereading, and sharing with a friend. *Cultivating Inspired Leaders* offers a pathway to follow complete with guideposts provided by the wit and wisdom of Bruce and Hodja to point the way. Leaders/managers—whether experienced or aspiring—will find it a valuable resource."

Barbara G. Ludwig
Professor & Department Chair
Ohio State University Extension

CULTIVATING INSPIRED LEADERS

CULTIVATING INSPIRED LEADERS

MAKING PARTICIPATORY MANAGEMENT WORK

BRUCE M. LANSDALE

DRAWINGS BY PAPAS

KUMARIAN
PRESS

Cultivating Inspired Leaders: Making Participatory Management Work

Published 2000 in the United States of America by Kumarian Press, Inc.,
14 Oakwood Avenue, West Hartford, Connecticut 06119-2127 USA.

Production and design by The Sarov Press, Stratford, Connecticut.
The text of this book is set in Berkeley 11/14.
Hodja drawings contributed by William Papas.

∞ Printed in Canada on acid-free paper by
Transcontinental Printing and Graphics, Inc.
Text printed with vegetable oil-based ink.

The paper used in this publication meets the minimum requirements
of the American National Standard for Information Sciences—Permanence of
Paper for Printed Library Materials, ANSI Z39.48–1984.

Library of Congress Cataloging-in-Publication Data
Lansdale, Bruce M., 1925–
    Cultivating inspired leaders : making participatory management work /
Bruce M. Lansdale ; drawings by Papas.
      p.   cm.
    Includes bibliographical references.
    ISBN 1–56549–110–6 (pbk. : alk. paper)
    1. Management—Employee participation. 2. Nonprofit organizations—
Management. 3. Organizational change. 4. Leadership. I. Papas, William. II. Title.

    HD5650 .L315 2000
    658.3'152—dc21
                                        99–087595

09 08 07 06 05 04 03 02 01 00   10 9 8 7 6 5 4 3 2 1

First Printing 2000

Dedicated To

Theo Litsas

(1900–62)

the most inspiring leader-manager
I have known.

He lived by his epitaph:

… whatever is true,
whatever is honorable,
whatever is just,
whatever is pure,
whatever is lovely,
whatever is gracious,
if there is any excellence,
if there is anything worthy of praise,
think about these things.

Philippians IV : 8

A Few Thoughts after September 1962

I feel that way about Theo too,
He taught me as much as any man.
When he was burned up in a car accident
I had to carry him back in a sheet.
He wasn't very heavy, but Lord, I cried afterwards,
So did two thousand other people at his funeral.
They cried because he laughed all his life
And got everything done,
Laughing!
We hauled a twenty-five-ton rock ten miles
And put it on the athletic field.
We put his name on it.
A friend wrote a dystich
"Rock like thy faith,
And like it, unbudgeable, thy works,
Theodore Litsas." (Lansdale 1979)

B.M.L.

CONTENTS

FOREWORD

There is no greater challenge among developing societies, whether among rural or urban populations, than cultivating what Bruce Lansdale refers to as inspired leader-managers. These are individuals, whether semi-illiterate or university graduates—from their own country or from farther afield—who wish to inspire others to attain higher levels of service and dedication to their fellow human beings.

How common it is to observe individuals who are inspiring leaders lacking in management skills, or administrative managers who lack the inspiration as leaders to influence those with whom they are working. Bruce has wisely chosen the phrase *inspired leader-managers*. It is not enough for those who are leaders to seek managerial skills or for the managers to cultivate leadership. These qualities must grow side by side to create in these individuals what is referred to in this book as inspired leader-managers.

I began my career in international development at the American Farm School in Greece in 1975 under Bruce's tutelage as a volunteer just out of college. My job was to operate a small-scale demonstration dairy unit and to train village youth in its operation and management. We began a new program called Summer Work Activities Program (SWAP) for college students and graduates from the developed and developing countries—my first endeavor at training leader-managers for development, under Bruce's leadership.

A few years later while I was serving in Tanzania, I arranged for West Virginia University to invite Bruce to study the integration of Tanzanian secondary agricultural schools with newly organized adult short-course training centers. The seminar that he conducted at the completion of his study became the basis for his original book, *Master Farmer: Teaching Small Farmers Management*, a book I have frequently used in university classes.

At Oregon State University, where he was appointed as Courtesy Professor following his retirement from the American Farm School, he undertook a needs assessment survey for us at the Agricultural University of Tirana in Albania. This led to a five-year project in training inspired leader-managers among the faculty and administration of Albanian agricultural schools which revolutionized secondary agricultural schools in the country.

Since his retirement he has traveled worldwide conducting seminars on cultivating inspired leader-managers, a number of them with my graduate students and fellow faculty members, where he has proven himself as an inspiring participatory leader.

This book is an outgrowth of these seminars. It should be required reading for all those working in the field of development. It is a practical as well as inspiring manual for all those dedicated to serving others either as volunteers or as professionals. I recommend it highly for individual reading, for courses, or for seminars on development designed for those seeking to manage private voluntary agencies at home or NGOs abroad.

David Acker
Director, International Agriculture
Programs
Iowa State University
Ames, Iowa

ACKNOWLEDGMENTS

One day an illiterate neighbor brought Hodja a poorly scribbled letter to read for him. When Hodja complained that it was illegible, the man accused him of being unworthy of the "turban of wisdom" that he wore. Hodja was furious at the insult and thrust the turban on his neighbor's head. "Here," he shouted, "you wear it and see if you can read the letter!"

"So, you wear the hat!"

Several generations of American Farm School Trustees, staff, and trainees have given me a lifetime education. But it was only after I retired at the age of sixty-five that I realized how much they had taught me and how much more there was to learn. When the University of Thessaloniki granted me an Honorary Doctorate in Agriculture, I pointed out that normal human beings earn a Ph.D. in thirty-six months. "Only if you are, as the Greeks say, a *boubounas*, or dumb baboon, can it take you forty-three years to earn one." How grateful I am to the Faculty of the Aristotelian University for the honor and for all they taught me over four decades.

"Growing old I keep learning," Plato quoted Solon as saying (Platonis Opera), and I am grateful to the multitude of my professors from all walks of life. True teachers always find time to offer insights and recognize that their interruptions are their work. It is impossible for me to acknowledge individually the many institutional administrators, extension workers, home economists, teachers at all levels, village and city residents, men and women alike, on five continents who have been so generous with their knowledge and their time.

One indispensable contributor to this book, who is believed to have been born between the thirteenth and fifteenth centuries, has so many names that he is difficult to identify. In Iran and much of the Arab world he is known as Mulla Nasredin; in Egypt as Goha; and in Turkey (where he is reputed to have been buried) as Nasredin Hodja. Muslims, Hindus, Christians, and Jews quote him, often with the conviction that his tales are part of their own religious tradition.

Children delight in Hodja's amusing stories, adults are impressed by his wisdom, teachers are interested in his philosophy, and theologians seek to understand his Sufi mysticism. His tales have taught me to laugh at myself in the most frustrating situations—a vital lesson for any development worker whether in the smog, noise, and congestion of the inner city or the pervading poverty of many marginal areas of the world. But reading Hodja stories is a poor substitute for listening to them beside the hearth in a peasant's hut or exchanging them for hours in a village coffee shop: experiences that are slowly disappearing in Greece along with the vanishing peasant. It is my hope that a sampling of his tales will arouse the reader's interest in learning more about him. To that end, I have included a listing of interesting books about Hodja in a bibliography at the end of this book.

The Bill Papas drawings of Hodja and Greek peasants who have been so much a part of his life and mine express the love and compassion that we both feel for them. His illustrations in *Tales of the Hodja* (Downing 1964), published more than thirty years ago, have brought my friend Hodja to life for our children, grandchildren, nieces, and nephews over the years. "Tell us a Hodja story, Papou," cry our grandchildren from Honduras, almost as soon as we arrive. I would like to thank Bill Papas for illustrating this book in a way that recreates peasants in their natural environment far more effectively than can the written word.

Nasredin Hodja, peasants, urban community leaders, and teachers around the world inspired a myriad of disjointed ideas that are the basis of this book. In an earlier book, *Master Farmer: Teaching Small Farmers Management* (Lansdale 1986), I attempted to share our experience at the American Farm School in training managers for rural development. This book is an effort to share a new set of observations which have convinced me of the importance of participatory management as the most important element of the art of managing voluntary organizations. I am particularly grateful to Robert Chambers, Niels Röling, and W. Edwards Deming, who helped me understand the value of this approach in becoming an inspiring leader-manager.

The reader will discover that this book ascribes a spiritual dimension to participatory management in voluntary organizations. Among my many legacies in taking over the directorship of the American Farm School from two generations of the House family, there was *A Devotional Diary* by J. H. Oldham.

This pocket volume, first published in 1925, had been a constant companion for the Houses during their morning meditations. A sprinkling of quotations from Oldham's *Diary* in this book provides nuggets of wisdom garnered from his readings over fifty years in India and the U.K.

During the 1960s my wife, Tad, and I made a study of "Who is in Command" in the Greek family for the Modern Greek Studies Association. A village priest whom we interviewed replied without a moment's hesitation, "Oh, the man is the head of the family!" But after a brief pause he added, "But the woman is the neck and decides which way the head should turn." I am most grateful not only to one neck, but to several.

Tad not only helped write this book—she also inspired many parts of it and has often been an integral part of many of the thoughts expressed. Two other "necks," Debbie Ellickson-Brown and Randall Warner, have kept my head facing in the right direction, helping me adapt my thoughts into a form that I hope does not require Hodja's turban to be understood. Our son, David Lansdale, spent many hours poring over the original manuscript making a multitude of helpful suggestions. He and Stephen Koolpe encouraged me to cut it in half, for which the reader will no doubt be grateful. I owe a great debt of gratitude to my teacher and friend, Anton Luitingh, who has turned my ungrammatical scrawl into what I hope is a comprehensible document and to Elizabeth Kilpatrick who converted a hodge-podge of formats into a uniform style. Last, but not least, I am deeply indebted to my editor, Sherry Crunkilton, who encouraged me to complete "my rooster" and proceeded to convert all that had gone before into a publishable book.

The high cost of publishing a book of this kind which will be distributed on five continents made it necessary to place a prepublication order for 1500 copies. Income from the sale of some of these copies will revert to the Library Fund of the American Farm School. They will be made available to development workers in countries as diverse as Nepal, Nigeria, Egypt, Malawi, Albania, Bulgaria, Kosovo, and Honduras, as well as to volunteer workers going overseas from North America and Western Europe. I am most grateful to a small group of friends, primarily from Greece under the leadership of George Legakis, who have contributed to this prepublication order. They include Paul Condellis, George David, Kitty Kyriakopoulou, Pandelis Panteliadis, George Portolos, Gerasimos Vassilopoulos, and an anonymous American friend.

INTRODUCTION

One day a beggar smelled the appetizing odors of a goat being cooked on the spit outside the house of a rich miser. He sat down on a nearby stone and started eating his crust of bread, dreaming that he too was eating a roast, as he sniffed the goat. Just as the beggar was finishing, the rich man spied him and demanded payment for the smell of his goat. Following a lengthy argument the two were brought before Hodja, the judge. When he heard the story, Hodja asked the beggar if he had any money. Protesting, the poor man finally pulled out two coins to hand over. At that moment Hodja withdrew his hand and allowed the coins to drop on the floor. He then asked the rich man if he had heard the coins dropping on the stone floor. When the miser said he had, Hodja paused for a moment and replied, "May the sound of the poor man's coins be payment for the smell of the rich man's goat."

"May the sound of the coin be payment for the smell of the goat."

FOR WHOM IS THIS BOOK?

A MANAGEMENT DEFINITION

This is a book for leader-managers at all levels and particularly those in voluntary organizations working at home or abroad. It is not necessarily directed at top leader-managers, although I hope it will be helpful to them too. It is important to define what the terms "leader-managers" and "management" mean. Ita Hartnett, the Supervisor of Farm and Home Management in County Cork, Ireland, gave me the simplest definition I have heard:

> "Management is doing what you want with what you've got."

Using this explicit definition, the goal of leader-managers at all levels in any organization is to serve their customers, making best use of the human, material, and financial resources available to them. This applies to a voluntary organization, a business, a development agency, a school, a hospital, a religious organization, or any one of a myriad of informal groups such as families, voluntary associations, or others serving their fellow human beings. We must always be conscious of the sound of the coin *and* the aroma of the roasting goat.

WHO ARE THE LEADER-MANAGERS?

Leader-managers are the variety of individuals using the tools and techniques available to them to help formal and informal organizations accomplish their goals ("what they want with what they've got"). This is a book for:

- secretaries, receptionists, and maintenance personnel whose tools may be word processors, telephones, brooms, and vacuum cleaners *as well as their warm smiles.*
- teachers, social workers, church and other group workers whose tools may be their textbooks, blackboards, case histories, and notebooks *as well as their loving hearts.*
- bookkeepers, accountants, and storekeepers whose tools may be their computers, spreadsheets, and inventory cards *as well as their attentive ears, which listen carefully to those whose records they maintain.*
- technicians, electricians, and shop workers who apply their heads and hands to producing excellence *as well as their arms to embrace those with whom they work.*
- workers of every type and in every position who *believe that there is something greater to what they are doing than appears in material form and wish to share this belief with their associates.*
- Trustees, ministers, CEOs, who, when they ponder policy, programs, and budgets *seek to use their head, their heart, and their spirit to serve their organization and their fellow men.*

LABORERS, TECHNICIANS, OR ARTISTS?

André Malraux, French writer, art historian, and advisor to several French presidents, provides the basis for describing individuals to whom this book is addressed:

> He (or she) who works with his hands is a laborer.
> He who works with his hands and his head is a technician.
> He who works with his hands, his head, and his heart is an artist.

Malraux might be adapted to read:

> Those who manage with their mind are *administrators*.
> Those who manage with their mind and their heart are *leader-managers*.
> Those who manage with their mind, their heart, *and* their soul are *inspired and inspiring leader-managers*.

LEADER-MANAGER CHARACTERISTICS

THREE CATEGORIES OF LEADER-MANAGERS

This is a book about becoming an inspired and inspiring leader-manager, regardless of position in an organization. Such individuals see their role as participants in the management process, working with associates, developing leadership skills among those around them, and cultivating managerial skills within themselves and fellow team members.

Three distinctions are made among categories of leader-managers:

1. *Administrators.* Traditional managers manage by right, privilege, or appointment. They have an understanding of planning, organizing, leading, controlling, and adjusting applied primarily in an authoritarian fashion. They base their authority on the position to which they have been appointed.

2. *Leader-managers.* Administrators who are capable of leading those with whom they are associated in a participatory fashion. They are eager to cultivate leadership among staff, volunteers and customers with whom they are associated (Chapters 3 to 8).

3. *Inspired and inspiring leader-managers.* Those who have themselves been inspired by others in their lives. Inspired leader-managers have a sense of dedication to their organization, to their associates, and a commitment to a spirit within themselves (Chapter 9). These individuals may, however, lack the self-confidence or the ability to inspire others. It is the inspiring leader-managers who are eager to share their inspiration with associates and customers of their organization (Chapter 10).

THE MANAGEMENT PYRAMID

Managers operate on four levels, as illustrated in the diagram on the next page. They begin at the bottom as administrators and progress through experience. Some of them never move to higher levels, spending their careers in one particular category while associates continue to rise in the pyramid.

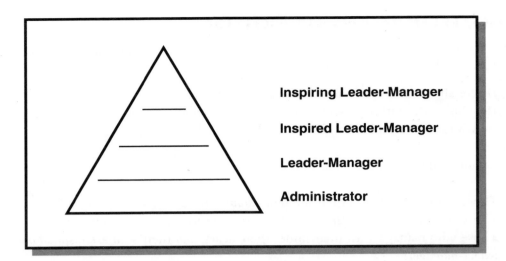

Inspiring Leader-Manager

Inspired Leader-Manager

Leader-Manager

Administrator

METAMORPHOSIS

The process of emergence and growth from the level of administrator to that of inspiring leader-manager is not unlike the metamorphosis of the butterfly from egg to larva, to pupa, and finally butterfly. As any inspiring leader-manager will ascertain, this process is every bit as challenging and often as agonizing as that of the butterfly (described below). As the author of the story concludes,

"Without the struggle, there are no wings!"

Most administrators acquire the confidence of leader-managers. Some in turn apply their spiritual selves to grow into inspired leader-managers and finally into inspiring leader-managers as they seek to inspire others. Those who grow through the process attest to the mental, emotional, and spiritual struggle involved. They also recognize how vital it is that individuals must undergo their own metamorphosis. The role of the inspiring leader-manager is limited to that of the midwife, providing advice, guidance, and inspiration. Only by themselves can butterflies shape their identity as they emerge from the cocoon.

A family once watched a butterfly squeeze itself slowly and painfully through a tiny hole it had chewed in the cocoon. After lying exhausted, the butterfly finally flew off on its beautiful wings. Distressed by the painful experience they observed, the family decided to help another butterfly by carefully slicing the cocoon. But the second butterfly never did sprout wings. A scientist friend explained that the struggle to emerge from the small hole pushes liquids from deep inside the butterfly's body cavity into the microscopic capillaries in the wings. Here they harden to complete the healthy and beautiful adult butterfly.

THE BACKGROUND OF THIS BOOK

Experiences and observation in many corners of this world over the past fifty years have inspired some thoughts about management practices. They have grown out of forty-three years working as a manager at the American Farm School with young people and adults from all over Greece and with trainees and visitors from around the globe. Usually we are able to perceive our own organization and its problems more clearly from the position of an outsider rather than from within.

As we attempt to measure our effectiveness as leaders of voluntary organizations, we must realize that "success" is measured by very different criteria. According to Peter Drucker, the most distinguished writer on management in the United States during the past century, "the 'non-profit' institution's 'product' is a *changed human being*." He goes on to question how we can measure our effectiveness as leaders within these organizations when "they do not have a conventional *bottom line*"(Drucker 1990, xiv). It is the customers who must measure the bottom line whether they are those who are being served or those who are serving. Only by constantly evaluating each other or themselves can leader-managers at all levels determine whether they are effectively contributing to *changing human beings*.

NIKOKIRIS MANAGERS

How do you teach managers within organizations to manage when they do not understand what management means? We discovered a partial solution in Greek by identifying the word *nikokiris* describing an individual who is "on top of things," capable of effective planning, organizing, leading, controlling, and adjusting to changing circumstances. The closest word in English is "a winner."

How could we find an equivalent word in Albanian, Nepalese, Spanish, Nigerian, Bulgarian, Ethiopian, and a variety of African dialects in countries where we worked? We could not. The answer was to use the word *nikokiris* in the original Greek. The tale of how we helped trainees to remember the word in such diverse places as Nepal, Honduras, and the United States, to mention but a few, is described in Chapter 2. It was a Honduran trainee who related the word *nikokiris* to the crowing of a rooster. "This morning," he announced, "I heard the rooster crow, and will always remember the word '*NIKOKIRIS!*'".

With 150,000 words in the Random House Dictionary, the reader may wonder why the English lan-

NEE-KO-KEE-REES!!

guage needs one more word. There may be several English words that approach the meaning of the Greek word *nikokiris*, but none of them really do it justice. This is particularly true in its broader interpretation, which incorporates being a leader-manager, a winner, a master craftsman, and the master of one's own destination. *Nikokiris* are individuals dedicated to quality in what they produce, to quality of life, and to quality of spirit.

THE LEADER-MANAGER AS A POLKA PLAYER

We still had not discovered an answer to the question, "What makes the leader-manager manage?" until we met with a group of dairy farmers in Greece several years ago. They understood *nikokiris*, because they each knew who the *nikokiris* were in their village and what their characteristics were. When we started talking "management" to them, however, it was as unintelligible as *nikokiris* had been to visitors from abroad. Here, too, we discovered a solution. "We are going to teach your cows to dance a POLKA," I announced to twenty-five quizzical faces. "Oh come on, you crazy Amerikanos!" said one of the group. They knew the polka was a Polish dance, but what relationship did it have to their cows? We put the answer on the blackboard in English and in Greek:

P	**PLANNING**	**PROGRAMATISMOS**
O	**ORGANIZING**	**ORGANOSI**
L	**LEADING**	**LAMBRI IGESIA**
K	**K(C)ONTROLLING**	**KONTROL**
A	**ADJUSTING**	**ANAPROSARMOGI**

All that remained was a discussion of how they could become more effective *nikokiris* by improving their approach to each of the five steps in the POLKA. A year later when they came back for a refresher course they were all pointing their finger at their chest saying, "Ego *nikokiris*" (I am a *nikokiris*!) When I asked them what else they remembered from the year before, they replied almost in unison, "POLKA! POLKA! POLKA!" One participant even suggested that his cows had learned to dance the polka! What more could we ask for?

I owe a deep debt of gratitude to Macedonian dairy farmers and seminar participants in many corners of the world for helping me to gain a better understanding of how the POLKA works. This is but a tiny sample of a multitude of individuals on five continents, marginal landholders and inner city residents alike, who have convinced us that the solutions to their problems lie within themselves and their communities.

THREE PRIORITIES

The term "leader" throughout this book is used primarily to describe the characteristics of a manager who is also a capable leader who might best be referred to as a leader-manager. More specifically, "leader" describes the qualities of a participatory or democratic manager, one whose goal it is to instill principles of democratic and participatory leadership.

Three priorities should be high on the list of leader-managers for their organization:

1. Continual leadership and leader-manager training at all levels.
2. The establishment of a focus on participatory quality management at every level.
3. An approach that gives all the staff and volunteers a sense that they are an integral part of the management team. This should begin with the janitor, receptionist, or gardener and go to the very top rung on the administrative ladder.

The qualities of the leader-manager are discussed in considerable detail in Chapter 6.

THE CHALLENGE OF THIS BOOK

There are ten specific characteristics which inspiring leader-managers need to cultivate as they progress from administrators to leader-managers, to inspired leader-managers, and finally to inspiring leader-managers. It is our hope that the qualities listed below will be of aid to aspiring leader-managers, should they make them a part of their management philosophy:

1. The challenge of recognizing customers as our most important concern (Chapter 1).
2. The values inherent in becoming an inspired leader-manager (Chapter 2).
3. The significance of a participatory approach to management (Chapter 3).
4. The value of planning as a participatory technique (Chapter 4).
5. The role of process as a vital dimension of organizing (Chapter 5).
6. The importance of spirit as an integral part of leadership in an organization (Chapter 6).
7. The significant contribution of staff at all levels to the process of control (Chapter 7).
8. The role of dynamic equilibrium in maintaining balance in vibrant programs (Chapter 8).
9. The contribution of inspired leader-managers in cultivating prosperity of spirit (Chapter 9).
10. The illusive qualities contributed by inspiring leader-managers to associates (Chapter 10).

THREE SOUNDS TO A STAR

Managers under the influence of inspiring leaders throughout the organization discover, when working in small teams or groups, that they are able to carry the concept of quality of management to a new dimension—the spiritual level. This quality of human relationships, often referred to at the American Farm School as "the Spirit of Dr. House," is expressed by Robert Browning's metaphor in his *Dramatis Personae* entitled "Abt Vogler" (Oldham 1959).

"Out of three sounds it frames not a fourth—but a star!"

FROM MOUNTAIN PEAK TO DESERT

Brother David Steindl-Rast, the Zen-inspired Benedictine monk, speaks of the two-step process of contemplation that leads to a peak experience as the "visionary ascent into the cloud that covers the mountain" as well as the descent into the desert, "there to realize the vision step by step" (Steindl-Rast 1994, 340). Are not our efforts as inspiring leader-managers of voluntary organizations but an extension of a monastic world? Our challenge is to help our associates implement what we have envisioned on the mountaintop when we work together in the desert.

Only when our management becomes participatory:
when the helper and the helped become one as a team,
the manager and the employee regard each other as companions,
the guide and the guided lead each other,
when we discern that we have encapsulated our common aspirations,
and that we are in and out of each others' dreams,
only then can we discover moments when
the rooster's crow turns into a nightingale's song.

CONCENTRATE ON CUSTOMERS

- What do we mean by quality in a service organization?

- Who are the enduring leader-managers of service organizations?

- What do we mean by the spiritual dimension of an organization?

"Tell me the secret of how you gave away the coin so easily."

For many years Hodja coveted a priceless gold coin owned by a simple uneducated monk who lived in a hermitage high above the village. Finally one day he decided to climb the hill and demand the coin which he felt rightfully belonged to him as the religious leader, judge, and teacher.

After a two-hour climb, he knocked on the monk's door and demanded the coin, "Since I am the most educated and wiser, I should have the coin."

To Hodja's amazement the humble monk dug into a trunk and handed the coin to Hodja, who was so surprised that he barely thanked the monk. As he headed down the hill, he happily fondled his prized possession.

Two hours later, the monk's meditation was disturbed by another knock on the door. He was taken aback to see Hodja a second time. "Take the coin back," said the Mulla, "but I want you to give me something far more valuable. Tell me the secret of how you gave the coin away so easily."

Inspired leader-managers of service organizations are ones who have discovered the secret of freely giving away their coin, whether it is experience, knowledge, technical skills, their vision, or their wisdom. For more than forty years, a group of staff at the American Farm School in Greece had been seeking to identify the characteristics of successful leader-managers at all levels in an organization. Hodja's eagerness to give back the gold coin in return for something far more priceless may provide a partial answer. We eventually identified three elements that play a vital role in the success of an organization:

1. The quality of the organization's service as evaluated by its customers.
2. Capable leader-managers (both staff and volunteers).
3. A unifying inspirational vision which clarifies its objectives (the "Vision Factor").

QUALITY DEVELOPMENT

THE MEANING OF SUCCESS

In the fall of 1990, a group of ten met in the mountains of Nepal, in the shadow of the 5,000- to 8,500-meter peaks of the Annapurna Range. Most were young Nepalese development workers who had invited my wife, Tad, and me to lead a week-long seminar. We began by discussing "success." What is it? Who should measure it? We listed several potential evaluators:

■ The sponsors and contributors?

■ The parent organization?

■ Those who use the organization's facilities?

■ The director and the managing committee?

■ The development workers acting as managers?

■ Their associates in the organization?

■ The village people whom they were there to help?

What is the standard by which and by whom the "success" of a service organization is measured and who measures it? Is it the ability to attract publicity, famous sponsors, and large donations? How often do service organizations, looking for a way to help, begin by deciding among themselves whom they will serve and in what direction they are going to take their clients?

We searched for an equivalent for "success" in the business world that speaks of "maximizing profits" as the ultimate measure. Lester Thurow, Dean of the Massachusetts Institute of Technology School of Management, argues that a successful business is one which *maintains satisfied customers*." If a business maximizes its profits, it might succeed for five years; if it seeks satisfied customers, it should continue as a successful enterprise indefinitely.

Customers, above all else, are not pawns on a chessboard, inanimate objects to be manipulated. They are vital individuals with ideas, desires, visions, and hopes. Our job is to help them realize their dreams—*their* dreams, not *ours*. This is a large group we are attempting to keep satisfied. We can only expect to succeed if everyone in the organization identifies customer satisfaction as his or her top priority. When we were in Nepal, we saw a small sign about customers on the wall of a bookstore in Katmandu. The

WHAT IS A CUSTOMER?

- A customer is the most important person in any business.

- A customer is not dependent on us, we are dependent on her.

- A customer is not an interruption of our work. He is the purpose of it.

- A customer does us a favor when she comes in. We are not doing her a favor by attending to her needs.

- A customer is part of our business, not an outsider.

- A customer is not just an object of our service organization's program. He is a human being with feelings and deserves to be treated with respect.

- A customer is a person who comes to us with her needs and her wants. It is our job to help her attain them.

- A customer deserves the most courteous attention we can give him. He is the lifeblood of this and every business. He pays our salary. Without him we would have to close up.

- *Don't ever forget it!*

statement above, attributed to Ghandi, provided a vivid description of customers and their expectations. It has been adapted for "customers" of service organizations.

LEADER-MANAGERS IN DEVELOPMENT

Our group also sought to define development as it related to service organizations. During my forty-three years of involvement in the American Farm School, I discovered the best definition of this process while doing volunteer work in Nepal. It was in a stimulating book on "Participatory Development" by Keith Leslie and Krishna Sob, directors of Save the Children/USA in Nepal:

> "Development occurs not simply when technical improvements occur, but more importantly, when people become critically aware of their own situation and, whenever necessary, are ready to change it" (Leslie and Sob 1990).

The onus for development is on local leaders and the residents of the neighborhood or community as well as on the development workers. In this sense, development consists of technical improvements coupled with the creation or expansion of critical awareness among those being served and their readiness to change.

We agreed on "prosperity" as a primary goal of development, but not the dictionary definition that is "the condition of prospering: success or wealth." The essential element of prosperity is quality of spirit—a deep-seated spiritual satisfaction in being alive. Beyond financial return, prosperity includes family rewards, social rewards, and spiritual rewards—but as part of the *process*, not the *destination*.

"He who knows he has enough is rich."—Balinese Proverb

THE LEADER-MANAGERS

PROFESSIONAL LEADER-MANAGERS

Our small group in the Himalayas tried to determine who were the "leader-managers" for their organization. Was it the chairperson of the board? Their contributors? Their financial managers? Their fund raisers? Their managing director? The field workers? The village leaders? We decided that they are all leader-managers.

Orathi Ard-am, an inner-city worker in Bangkok, shared the following thoughts about characteristics and viewpoints that contribute to effectiveness on the part of leader-managers of service organizations:

- Be active in your support. Don't approach it as an academician or theoretician.
- Be a catalyst whose first challenge is to make yourself superfluous as soon as possible.
- Do not force an innovation on people if they do not want it.
- Identify and assist local leaders who will provide the lasting momentum for sustainable development.

Many professional leader-managers have a tendency to dominate volunteer leader-managers. They feel that "things will be done better and faster" if they are in charge. In the short run, this may be true. In the long run, only those changes adopted by the volunteers will have a lasting impact. The short-term approach may appear more efficient. The professional must ask, however, "Will my approach be effective in the long term?"

In accordance with a concept introduced by management guru Peter Drucker, *efficient* managers introduce innovations *they* want and make sure they are implemented. *Effective* leader-managers help their customers identify *their* needs and accomplish what *they* want.

THE INTERRELATEDNESS OF SERVICE ORGANIZATIONS AND CUSTOMERS

There is an obvious difference between Gandhi's bookstore customer and the service organization's customer. In service organizations, the active participation of the customer is necessary in order for the "business" of the service organization to be successful. Every product of a service organization should be custom-made and requires the continuous active involvement of both the "business" and "customers" in order to be successful.

This requires that all those involved in the organization, whether professionals or volunteers, think of themselves as leader-managers. Volunteer leader-managers are responsible for developing and maintaining the organizational structure among the organization's customers. They are part of the local community or other groups being served. Professional leader-managers, the service organization's employees, are responsible for maintaining the organizational structure and creative process to assure that the volunteers' goals are being accomplished.

THE MIDWIFE

John Heider provided a most helpful challenge to leader-managers of service organizations in his book, *The TAO of Leadership*. To paraphrase him:

> The wise leader-manager does not intervene unnecessarily. His or her presence is felt, but often the group runs itself. Imagine that you are a midwife; you are assisting at someone else's birth. Do good without show or fuss. Facilitate what is happening rather than what you think ought to be happening. If you must take the lead, lead so that the mother is helped, yet still is free and in charge. When the baby is born, the mother will rightly say "We did it ourselves," as the midwife unobtrusively walks away.

VOLUNTEER LEADER-MANAGERS

Professional leader-managers of service organizations speak of the "real" leader-manager as the insider, the farmers, the slum dwellers, the women, the mothers—the members of the community who will sustain the momentum long after all of the professionals have gone. These individuals are both customers and a part of the service organization who should be participating as an integral part of the process.

Tad and I met such a person, Hari Pun, quite by chance in Goropani, a small town 9,600 feet above sea level in the Himalayas with more than twenty trekking lodges. It was approachable only by several hours of trekking. He was the Chairperson of the Forestry Committee for ACAP (Annapurna Conservation Area Program). Remember, when you read what he said, that Nepal is one of the ten poorest countries in the world and that it is the lowest in literacy and the highest in infant mortality according to the ranking of the World Bank. The following is a summary of the ten goals which this man, Hari Pun, described in his own words for us:

1. We must protect the natural animals from the hunters, and keep the tigers, deer, monkeys, wolves, wildcat, bear alive. They will only bother you if they have babies.

2. We must stop cutting down our trees and replant rhododendrons. Without the trees we have no oxygen, no water. When I show them a live leaf and a dead one they understand, but they forget. We have more meetings. They need more knowledge. We have to build up trees. We have to love trees—not women, not men—all people must learn to build up trees.

3. We want to organize reading and writing classes for wives and illiterate children—but not in the monsoon season when we cannot travel.

4. We must introduce sanitation and cleanliness—clean our nails, wash our hands. My mother-in-law doesn't want to go to the outhouse—in the old days, she thought that going to the toilet outside with the wildlife around was beautiful. But we must change.

5. Our children want to go to school, but the parents don't have enough money—but now the government is planning new ideas for education. I am optimistic, but there was much corruption in the old government.

6. We are afraid that if people don't plant trees we will ruin the land and they will drive us out. We must save the trees. Everyone likes ACAP—maybe three or four houses do not come to our meetings.

7. (When we spoke of using foreign assistance, his voice rose.) Foreign aid needs three things—right money, right place, right use! Before it all went to the government and didn't come to the village. Only on radio we heard about United States Aid of $75,000,000, but it never came to the village.

8. We need one family of four—mother, father, two children—family planning, birth control pills, ministry of health center; women are interested, but it is difficult, it takes time—everything needs teaching.

9. We have no doctor. If you break a leg, I have to carry you for seventy-two hours. All our children are born at home.

10. Father and mother must learn to plan, to look at clothes, to look at the moneybox so that husband and wife can decide to build a new house. We learned and had our training from the grandfather.

Men like Hari Pun are a vital force in any community, but especially in one attempting to pull itself up by the bootstraps with no electricity, no running water, no road, and no vehicle of any kind. Wise outsiders will see themselves as catalysts and facilitators seeking to help Hari implement his program rather than trying to introduce one of their own. What does Hari Pun want from you and me, the leader-managers of our service organizations who are not part of the community? He wants anything that you can give in a secular way—resources, know-how, organization, but also something more, something bigger! The Hari Puns of this world want everything that the monk's gold coin will buy, but they also want to know the secret of how to give it away.

SPIRITUAL DIMENSIONS OF SERVICE ORGANIZATIONS

SERVICE, VOLUNTARY, AND DEVELOPMENT ORGANIZATIONS

The terms service, voluntary, and development are used interchangeably to describe the word organization throughout this chapter. An organization might simply be defined as two or more individuals working together toward a common goal. Webster defines the verb, volunteer, as "to offer (oneself or one's services) for some undertaking or purpose." Thus a service or voluntary organization is a group of two or more individuals offering their services for some undertaking or purpose. It defines develop as "to bring out the capabilities or possibilities." In this book, service, voluntary, and development organizations have as their goal to bring out the capabilities or possibilities of individuals, groups, or communities.

SPIRITUAL DIMENSIONS OF LEADER-MANAGERS

The real challenge for leader-managers, both insiders and those there to help, is to listen and to relate to customers. Perhaps a better word might be *integrate,* for which the Greek word is *afomiono,* which literally means "to make a part of myself." As important as listening is the involvement of our total self—the investment of our humanity. It cannot be "*just* a job." Hear the challenge of Albert Schweitzer, one of the greatest development workers of all time:

"Open your eyes and look for some person or some work for the sake of human beings that needs a little time, a little friendship, a little sociability, a little human toil. Search and see if there is not some place where you may invest your humanity" (Schweitzer 1959).

It can never be just a job—we must invest our total humanity. The Hari Puns of the world want us to climb out of our own ego, forget our self-centered identity and think of ourselves as truly loving those we are there to help.

The advice of former United Nations Secretary General Dag Hammarskjold to the successful leader-manager seeking to help others sheds further light on what is expected of us:

"When you have reached the point where you no longer expect a response, you will at last be able to give in such a way that the other is able to receive, and be grateful. When love has matured and, through a dissolution of the self into light, becomes a radiance, then shall the Lover be liberated from dependence upon the Beloved and the Beloved also be made perfect by being liberated from the Lover" (Hammarskjold 1964).

Hari Pun wants us to work *on his priorities at his pace*, not at ours, understand the meaning of quality of spirit *in his terms*, not ours, perhaps to speed up a bit on meeting *his* needs.

A TOTAL COMMITMENT

Leader-managers, whether working in an inner city near home or in the far corners of the world, think of their work as a total commitment. In order for these people to become a part of our lives, they must be as much our people as we are theirs. The Hari Puns want us to come closer to their culture, to their way of life, and in many ways to become one of them.

Hari Pun wants us to clarify our goal: Why are we here? To profit, make money, gain recognition? Or for the pure satisfaction of our work? We must make the distinction Erich Fromm describes in his book *To Have or to Be?* (Fromm 1988). Are we here for ourselves, to exist in a "having" mode, thinking in terms of our possessions and the salaries and other rewards we can gain? Or are we seeking a "being" mode, which involves giving of the self, helping to solve other people's problems as they see them, forgetting our rights, and being prepared to live at the level of local citizens? We must avoid having a possessive sense about "our" program, "our" goals, and "our" success. We should reach a point where we are able to hug the people we are helping with open arms, asking nothing in return but the reward they feel about their own accomplishments.

In the process, each one will inevitably be changed,

teachers as liberally as their students,

doctors as deeply as their patients,

nurses as much as the convalescents,

social workers as fundamentally as their clients,

extension agents as profoundly as farmers,

economists as much as those who become their statistics,

child welfare workers as emotionally as their charges,

YMCA, YWCA, or Scout leaders as powerfully as their young members,
church, synagogue, mosque, and temple leaders as spiritually as
their congregations.

Only when we have learned to give away every one of our gold coins, can we think of ourselves as inspired leader-managers of quality service organizations. We must not anticipate gratitude or recognition for our efforts. Rather we must seek to turn away from rewards toward giving for the simple satisfaction of what eventually becomes a spontaneous act.

In *The Book of Angels*, Armand Eisen quotes Alphonse de Lamartine:

"To love for the sake of being loved is human,
but to love for the sake of loving is angelic" (Eisen 1995).

We may never think in angelic terms, but surely we can learn to give of our love simply for the satisfaction of giving.

EVALUATE YOURSELF

- How can we distinguish effective leader-managers from ineffective ones at all levels in organizations?

- How and when should leader-managers, organizations, and their programs be evaluated?

- Who should evaluate service organizations and their leader-managers at any level?

"If the good say you are good . . ."

One day Hodja's apprentice gazed at him with admiration and perplexity. "Hodja," he said, "Everybody says you are good. Does that mean you are good?" "Not necessarily," counseled the wise man. "If they say you are bad, does that mean you are bad?" When Hodja said no, the youth asked his big question—"How can you tell, then, if you are good or bad?" Hodja thought for a moment stroking his beard. "I'll tell you, my friend. If the good people say you are good and the bad people say you are bad, that's when you are good." There was a long pause. "But you know how hard it is to tell which are the good and which are the bad!"

DISTINGUISHING BETWEEN NIKOKIRIS AND KAKOMIRIS

WHO ARE THE LEADER-MANAGERS?

Who are the true leader-managers in an organization or a community and what are their qualities? This was a subject of continual discussion over many years among the staff of the American Farm School as we analyzed the impact of the graduates on their villages. It became an even more relevant question as leaders were being selected by their fellow villagers to represent them at community development conferences coordinated by the School in Northern Greece.

Interestingly enough, the one word answer to this opening question in Greek was "*Nikokiris!*" *Nikokiris* had the leadership qualities to introduce change and also to gain acceptance of their new ideas. When we began conducting seminars outside Greece, trainees kept saying, "How can we possibly remember that word *nikokiris?*"

THE MANAGER AS ROOSTER—"NEEKOKEEREES!"

A Honduran seminar participant in a mountain town, Santa Barbara, provided a solution to remembering the word *nikokiris*. He came to us on the third morning of our seminar with a big smile. "I know what a *nikokiris* is!" he announced triumphantly. He had been awakened at dawn by a rooster and immediately understood what the cock was crowing: "NEEKOKEEREES!" he cried, proud to have found a way to remember the word. "NEEKOKEEREES!" he repeated, screeching just like a rooster.

He went on to describe the characteristics of the rooster as they related to a manager of a voluntary agency or a community leader. "He is the first one up in the morning. He is proud of who he is, what he does, and his relationship to his community. He is as dependable as an alarm clock, and appears to be systematic in his planning for the day. He is well organized and he is obviously the key leader respected by his flock. He maintains careful control of his extended family, but is willing to adjust to changing circumstances."

"She could even be a female rooster," he added sheepishly. Clearly our Honduran friend had been much inspired by the early morning crowing. As he finished his analysis he paused for a moment adding, "You know, I don't know what makes the rooster crow, but I am not sure what makes the manager manage either."

WHO EVALUATES?

No doubt leader-managers at all levels in service organizations ask themselves the same question, "Am I a winner or a loser?" In Hodja's terms, am I good or am I bad? Are there equivalent words in my native tongue for the Greek terms, *nikokiris* and *kakomiris*? Who decides whether I, or the organization with which I am associated, is *nikokiris* or *kakomiris*? How do you know "which are the good people and which are the bad?"

Development workers have long assumed that they themselves or other outside "experts" were the ones most qualified to evaluate a program. In contrast, those receiving advice or help were thought incapable of such judgment. Only in recent years have we accepted Hodja's wisdom in recognizing the difficulty in distinguishing "which are the good ones and which are the bad."

This chapter deals with four elements of the evaluation process:

1. Distinguishing between *nikokiris* and *kakomiris* managers.
2. Identifying *nikokiris* leader-managers for role models.
3. Prompting leader-managers, at all levels, to evaluate themselves and each other.
4. Contrasting *nikokiris* and *kakomiris* leader-managers.

NIKOKIRIS, KAKOMIRIS DISTINCTIONS

The Greek words *nikokiris* and *kakomiris*, distinguishing between two extreme types of individuals or organizations, play such a key role in this book that they deserve further clarification. Both *nikokiris* and *kakomiris* are used as nouns and as adjectives. As nouns in this book they are used in the plural.

1. The *nikokiris* (translated "the masters of their house") are the leaders in their community, respected by others for their judgment, leadership, and management skills. They initiate action, plan and organize their work effectively, often employing others, while taking advantage of every opportunity to improve the operation of their organization regardless of their position—whether they are the owners, managers, or employees. Neighbors, associates at work, and friends turn to them for support in times of crisis.

2. The *kakomiris* (literally translated as "the ill-fated ones") are the ones who are down on their luck or who have suffered some natural misfortune. They are much like the Kentucky mountaineer, Joe Bliftsick, in the old Al Capp cartoon, "Li'l Abner," popular in the United States three decades ago, who is always shown with a dark cloud over his head. Discussions with many individuals in Greece confirm the observation that the *kakomiris* almost always bring bad luck on themselves through lack of adequate planning or organization, even though they blame others for all their setbacks. Table 2.1 lists Greek phrases used by *kakomiris* in mid-twentieth-century Greece.

The self-evaluation form in Table 2.2 at the end of this chapter, as well as others throughout this book, will help leader-managers at all levels evaluate their performance. These *nikokiris/kakomiris* qualities provide criteria for evaluating the present status as well as a line or direction which will aid the positive growth of each individual being evaluated.

NIKOKIRIS ORGANIZATIONS

In Greece the concepts of *kakomiris* and *nikokiris* generally apply to individuals and families. The terms can be used just as well in discussing organizations and institutions. Many of the qualities and behavior patterns can be used to evaluate leader-managers at all levels in community development programs, schools, public health agencies, or any other voluntary organizations. It was with this observation in mind that a leader-manager self-evaluation form exploiting the extreme contracts of the *kakomiris* and *nikokiris* was compiled. The table provides a means for self-evaluation by the staff, volunteers, and customers of an organization. Obviously, no organization or institution can be totally *kakomiris* or *nikokiris* in every aspect of its operations. The evaluation of staff and customers is often closer to reality than that performed by skilled outside evaluators.

TABLE 2.1 Phrases used by *kakomiris* in mid-twentieth-century Greece with their literal and implied meanings (Lansdale 1986, 20).

GREEK PHRASE	LITERAL TRANSLATION	IMPLIED MEANING
Then ginete	It can't be done.	It hasn't been done before so it can't be done now.
Katalava, katalava	I understand, I understand.	I've got a much faster mind than you think.
Opou nanai erhetai	Any moment now.	Wherever he is (and I don't really know) he will be coming (and I'm not sure when).
Then birazi	It doesn't matter.	Don't bother me with details.
Then variese	I can't be bothered.	It doesn't make much difference, and I don't care.
To atimo	The dishonest thing.	It's the thing's fault for breaking down, not mine.
Na to skefto	Let me think about it.	Give me a chance to ask my wife what she thinks.
Xeris pios eim'ego?	Do you know who I am?	I'm as good as you are because I'm related to a VIP and don't you forget it.
Tha ta volepsoume	We'll take care of it.	I haven't really figured it out but don't you worry about it, I'll find a solution.
Tha se kanoniso	I'll fix you.	I'll get even with you if it's the last thing I do.

IDENTIFYING POTENTIAL NIKOKIRIS

NIKOKIRIS—BORN OR TRAINED?

Inner-city residents in industrialized societies and individuals in developing societies throughout the world have demonstrated their capacity to become successful managers capable of overcoming a variety of challenges inherent in poverty. Perceptive leader-managers of service organizations quickly realize that those in need of help are often eager to improve their own way of life and have the potential to do so. Too many voluntary organizations rely on external professionals to supply the required leadership rather than organizing community-based training programs. Local residents, the customers, become skeptical because outsider experts propose complicated solutions, if not outright wrong ones, which could be solved by locals if they were only consulted.

Can latent *nikokiris* be identified in the inner cities of wealthy countries or within poorer nations, among small businessmen, technicians, and farmers? Industrial managers recognize the value of training unskilled workers to become master technicians and successful entrepreneurs. It is important that corresponding training and in-service training programs must help these individuals among the poor and unemployed in every society. Institutional and in-service training programs must help these individuals to feel more positive about themselves. They should help them acquire the knowledge, competencies, and attitudes required for effective community leadership.

A NIKOKIRIS PHILOSOPHY

A *kakomiris* philosophy is based on "we'll decide if it's good when we finish." In contrast, the *nikokiris* think, "make every step right—every part of the procedure must live up to our measure of excellence." The leader-manager at all levels, the master craftsman, his technicians, his laborers, and apprentices must commit themselves to the standards of the organization, applying constant self-evaluation throughout. A *nikokiris* leader-manager realizes that he cannot dictate quality to his employees, but must look on them as associates who insist on *his* standards of excellence in *their* work. Ultimately *nikokiris* create a culture within their organization that inspires everyone to attain the same goal.

NIKOKIRIS EVALUATIONS

CONSTANT QUALITY CONTROL

It may seem surprising that the subject of evaluation is introduced in the second chapter of this book. Quality control and evaluation are usually performed by outside "experts" at the termination of a project. Among quality organizations, a fundamental tenet is, "Eliminate dependence on mass inspection." According to Deming, inspection with the aim of finding the bad products and throwing them out is considered *"too late, ineffective, costly"* (Walton 1986). Evaluation must be an integral part of an ongoing process, not an activity tacked on to the end. Quality should be a pervading philosophy that penetrates every level of the organization.

EVERYBODY SHOULD EVALUATE

Self-evaluation forms follow most chapters in this book. These will help individuals or groups evaluate where they think they are and where they would like to be. In filling out the forms, participants are given an opportunity to:

1. Identify where they stand on any quality and where they would like to be.
2. Determine the priority of changes to be made: since they cannot all be implemented at once.
3. Prepare an action plan (POLKA) to implement the changes.
4. Eliminate any qualities listed on the questionnaire that are not appropriate.
5. Add additional qualities that have not been included.

The self-evaluation form in Table 2.2 is based on evaluations of the Greek peasant. It is a personal evaluation, which can be used by managers at all levels about themselves. They can fill it out alone or ask a group of associates to do it with them. It can also be adapted to include a department or a whole organization.

Participants generally concur that a team effort is required to implement the desired changes through an organizational evaluation, as compared to individual self-evaluations. Where trustees, employees, volunteers, and customers take part in the evaluation and subsequent implementation, the sense of participatory accomplishment generates both a team spirit and a strong sense of pride.

HOW CAN LEADER-MANAGERS EVALUATE THEMSELVES?

The section that follows describes a series of contrasting characteristics among leader-managers at all levels. In order to avoid the reading of this section as a theoretical exercise, it is followed by a self-evaluation form which the reader is urged to fill out as suggested above. Each item in the next section has a corresponding line in Table 2.2 at the end of this chapter. Readers may want to turn to the table before reading the pages that follow. This will help them better understand the relationship between the next section and Table 2.2, which is based on the following instructions:

1. For each item listed in Table 2.2 on page 20, place an "X" on a scale of 1 to 5 to *show where you are* in a *kakomiris-nikokiris* rating based on pages 18 and 19.
2. Using the same scale of 1 to 5, place a "Y" *where you would like to be* on this scale.
3. In the Priority Column, prioritize each item listed by entering a number on a scale of 5 (top priority) to 1 (lowest priority) indicating the importance you give to the particular item. Using this technique, you can clarify your own priorities. If working as a group, the sum of the priorities for any single item can be added up, providing a "group feeling."
4. Draw a line through any item listed in Table 2.2 that you feel does not apply.
5. At the end of the form list other items that you think should have been listed and were not.
6. Having completed the exercise, prepare an action plan (POLKA) for items with high priorities.

NIKOKIRIS-KAKOMIRIS CONTRASTS

What are the qualities of individuals who are respected as *nikokiris* leader-managers? Many of these qualities are easier to identify from studying the behavior patterns and characteristics of those who are the antithesis of the *nikokiris*: the *kakomiris* leader-managers. The following analysis of these attributes provides the basis for Table 2.2. Readers may think through every quality listed and adapt or adjust them to their own situation.

The attributes to be evaluated are as follows:

Acquiring New Knowledge
The *kakomiris* leader-managers' false pride stands in the way of their seeking new knowledge: the *nikokiris* leader-managers continually seek to broaden their scope in relation to their environment.

Attitudes toward Associates
The *kakomiris* leader-managers are suspicious of others, ingratiating with superiors and overbearing with inferiors: the *nikokiris* leader-managers are respectful and confident in their relationship with associates.

Reaction to New Ideas
The *kakomiris* leader-managers are resistant to new ideas until they are proven effective: the *nikokiris* leader-managers are willing to test a new idea even though they may be cautious until it proves itself.

Problem-solving Approach
The *kakomiris* leader-managers jump to conclusions without analyzing a problem: the *nikokiris* leader-managers are careful in their analytical approach.

Clarity of Thinking
The *kakomiris* leader-managers are subjective and dismissive in their thinking at a personal level: the *nikokiris* leader-managers are objective and problem-oriented in their thinking.

Relationship with Associates
The *kakomiris* leader-managers tend to belittle or disparage their associates, especially in speaking to others about them: the *nikokiris* leader-managers look for the best in their associates and build a relationship of trust.

Emotional Stability
The *kakomiris* leader-managers are volatile and quick to show their temper: the *nikokiris* leader-managers are steady and dependable and control their anger even when they are sorely provoked.

Sense of Responsibility
The *kakomiris* leader-managers tend to blame others or fate when things go wrong: the *nikokiris* leader-managers accept responsibility for their mistakes.

Effective Planning
The *kakomiris* leader-managers have no clear short-, medium-, or long-term personal or organizational objectives: the *nikokiris* leader-managers have clear-cut goals motivated by a sense of vision.

General Organization
The *kakomiris* leader-managers' enterprise reflects poor organization: the *nikokiris* leader-managers' operation exhibits order and careful participatory organization.

Leadership Abilities
As leaders, *kakomiris* leader-managers are overbearing and critical: the *nikokiris* leader-managers know what they want and give lucid instructions to their workers. They in turn perform well, earning praise that inspires confidence and loyalty.

Record Keeping
The *kakomiris* leader-managers keep few records or none at all: the *nikokiris* leader-managers keep careful records that they study for further planning.

Consultation with Others
The *kakomiris* leader-managers tend to be rigid in changing circumstances: *nikokiris* leader-managers consult with their associates and are ready to adapt their plans to contrary opinions and interests under changing circumstances.

Having read the *kakomiris/nikokiris* contrasts in this section, readers are invited to evaluate themselves in Table 2.2 on the next page.

TABLE 2.2 Self-Evaluation Form

CHAPTER 2: EVALUATE YOURSELF Where are you as a leader-manager on the scale: *Kakomiris* (1) . . . to . . . *Nikokiris* (5)?						
TOPIC	1	2	3	4	5	PRIORITY
1. Acquiring new knowledge (page 18)						
2. Attitudes toward associates (page 18)						
3. Reaction to new ideas (page 18)						
4. Problem-solving approach (page 18)						
5. Clarity of thinking (page 18)						
6. Relationship with associates (page 18)						
7. Emotional stability (page 18)						
8. Sense of responsibility (page 18)						
9. Effective planning (page 19)						
10. Careful organization (page 19)						
11. Lucid leadership (page 19)						
12. Detailed record keeping (page 19)						
13. Consultation with others (page 19)						

(Numbers in parentheses refer to pages where subject is mentioned.)

1. For each topic, place an "X" under the 1, 2, 3, 4, or 5 to show where you think you are now as a leader-manager.
2. For each topic, place a "Y" under the 1, 2, 3, 4, or 5 to show where you would like to be.
3. Mark any item where the topic does not apply to your program "NA" (Not Applicable).
4. Under priority, enter a number on a scale from 5 (top priority) to 1 (lowest priority).
5. Identify three or four of your primary concerns on this theme and develop a "POLKA" plan of work to deal with them.
6. List other concerns, share them with your associates, and evaluate them as above.

APPLY PARTICIPATORY TECHNIQUES

- What are the components of participatory management?

- What is required of leader-managers in participatory organizations?

- How do "DOING TO," "DOING FOR," and "DOING WITH" relate to participatory management?

"The soup of the soup, of the soup,
of the soup of my friend's chicken!"

One day a childhood friend of Hodja's whom he had not seen in many years decided to pay him a visit. He chose his fattest hen, climbed on his donkey, and traveled for most of the day to reach the home of his delighted friend. While Hodja cooked the chicken, they had plenty of time to catch up on the "good old days," a discussion that lasted well into the night enriched by Hodja's tasty egg and lemon-boiled chicken soup. The next day when the friend returned to the village he regaled the coffee shop with tales of his visit to Hodja. "Do you suppose I could visit him?" asked a friend of the friend. When he was assured of Hodja's hospitable nature, the friend set off. Hodja welcomed him warmly as a friend of his friend, added some water to the soup and boiled up some of the leftover chicken. When a third friend arrived announcing that he was a friend of the friend of his friend, Hodja added a bit more water to the soup, dug out the last of the chicken and prepared still another repast. But when a fourth friend arrived and introduced himself, Hodja had but a half cup of the soup and some bones which he boiled as best he could, but alas, it was more boiled water than chicken soup. "What is this?" asked the surprised visitor who had heard tales of the great feasts from his friends. "Ah, my good friend, of the friend, of the friend, of my friend," responded the Hodja with a wry smile, "this is the soup, of the soup, of the soup, of the soup of my friend's chicken!"

IDENTIFY THE COMPONENTS OF MANAGEMENT

KEEP THE FLAVOR ALIVE AT ALL LEVELS

One of the principal goals of this book is to help leader-managers of service organizations acquire the skills needed to make the soup of the soup of the soup as tasty as the original soup. It is so easy to show concern for next door neighbors, childhood playmates, or longtime friends. It is so difficult to demonstrate a comparable commitment to others who live in distant countries or neighborhoods or who are far removed in the hierarchy within the organization. We may be willing to offer the soup of the soup to a friend of a friend, but more distant relationships are more difficult to cultivate, especially when there is a language or cultural barrier.

Top leader-managers of service organizations find similar obstacles in relating to staff several rungs below them on the organizational ladder. Like Hodja, the best we are willing to offer is the watered down "soup of the soup of the soup." The essential element of participatory management demands mutual respect and commitment on the part of giver and receiver at all levels.

BE SURE THE VISION PERCOLATES

The major challenge of an inspired leader-manager is to assure that the flavor of his or her vision of management and its expression within the organization percolate through all levels of management down to employees at the very lowest echelon and from all of them to every customer. Customers, employees, and volunteers within the organization must sense that they are in direct touch with top management. Each one must feel a sense of direct contact with the leader-managers through their contact person in the organization.

APPLY THE POLKA ACRONYM

The top levels of management must so inspire their associates at all levels that each individual will feel committed to reflect the essence of the thinking at the top. "What do they mean by management?" these individuals often ask. Employees strive to accept management responsibilities, yet they are not entirely clear what management or manager really means. We chose to introduce an acronym, POLKA, in Greece because no equivalent word for management exists in Greek or in most other languages. It might be helpful even to native English speakers.

Using the word POLKA as an acronym, we arrive at the five components of management:

PLANNING

ORGANIZING

LEADING

K(C)ONTROLLING

ADJUSTING

BUILD THE POLKA FROM THE BOTTOM UP

The POLKA is an essential foundation on which leader-managers at all levels can build. It can be used within a service organization as well as with the customers of an organization. Chapters 4 to 8 are devoted to clarifying how these components can be applied to more effective management of participatory organizations. How do we attain our goal in a participatory sense? Two wise men provided an answer.

W. Edwards Deming was the primary force in developing the concept of "Total Quality_Management" (TQM) in Japan and subsequently in the United States. This approach to management, based primarily on a participatory approach, had a profound impact on increasing productivity in industry, and subsequently among service organizations as well. Deming's philosophy of management was based on a relatively elementary approach. In Deming's terms:

> "Hammering away at the importance of anticipating the desires of customers, winning the trust and involvement of employees and constantly improving both processes and products . . ." (Walton 1986).

Robert Chambers's thinking, in his book *Rural Development, Putting the Last First*, applies every bit as much to working with the urban poor or managing service organizations as it does to working in the Third World. His primary contention was:

> "Instead of starting with the knowledge, problems, analysis and priorities of scientists, start[ing] with the knowledge, problems, analysis and priorities of farmers, farm families [and the urban poor], described as "farmers-first" ["inner-city residents first"] (Chambers 1983).

Both of these dynamic men recognize the importance of building on the needs felt by the customers while at the same time recognizing that each employee or volunteer has a major contribution to make as a manager.

RECOGNIZE THAT POLKAS ARE NEVER STATIC

A POLKA is seldom static, for it is an expression of a process undergoing constant change. Ideally it might best be expressed as a three-dimensional pyramid or a Buckminster Fuller dome in tension with overlapping triangles of varying sizes and shapes, each of which relates to the other. An overall POLKA clarifies the strategic management process of an organization. There must also be a multitude of specific action plans—POLKAs of their own which contribute to their smooth operation.

Limitations of the written word make it necessary to transcribe POLKA in a straight line. Individuals responsible for formulating them might better think of them as pyramids:

This specifies "who is at the top of the pyramid" as a coordinator of any single activity. It might even be better to express this relationship as an inverted pyramid:

This reminds leader-managers in the "L" that they are there to serve and coordinate rather than dominate the management process.

UNDERSTAND THE INTERRELATEDNESS OF POLKAS

The pyramid in Figure 3.1 expresses some of the complexities and the interrelatedness of the many-sided and multidirectional POLKAs involved in the process of management. Committees or individuals working in consultation with their associates must focus on particular problems, analyze each one, and develop a plan to resolve them and then implement the plan. Vital to each POLKA is an agreement on who is in the "L" position—"Whose POLKA is it?" Eventually, all staff members and volunteers will reach a point where they feel they are parts of "their own" POLKAs and can identify who is at the top of the pyramid in their particular effort.

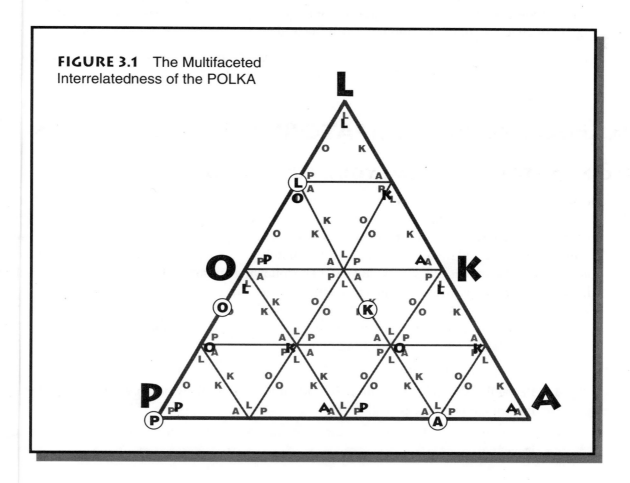

FIGURE 3.1 The Multifaceted Interrelatedness of the POLKA

WHO IS "ONEBODY?"

This is a story about four people named *Everybody, Somebody, Anybody,* and *Nobody*. There was an important job to be done and *Everybody* was sure that *Somebody* would do it. *Anybody* could have done it, but *Nobody* did it. Now *Somebody* got angry about that because it was *Everybody*'s job. *Everybody* thought *Anybody* could do it, but *Nobody* realized that *Everybody* wouldn't do it. It ended up that *Everybody* blamed *Somebody* when *Nobody* did what *Anybody* could have done! And all they needed from the beginning was "*ONEBODY*!"

In healthy organizations, POLKAs are not only interrelated to each other. They may be in a state of strain among the five components. Tension between overlapping POLKAs within an organization can also be a challenge. Where the leader-manager at the top of any pyramid has been identified, this potential source of conflict can be changed from unhealthy competitiveness to close cooperation growing out of effective communication between the leaders.

Lacking clarity in defining this responsibility, whose POLKA it is, is bound to result in the oft-quoted tale of the "Four Friends" related in "Who Is Onebody?"

MANAGING PARTICIPATORY ORGANIZATIONS

BEGIN BY LEARNING FROM YOUR CUSTOMERS

A picture of Gandhi on the cover of the paperback edition of E. F. Schumacher's *Small is Beautiful, Economics as if People Mattered*, shows him in his simple *dhoti* (Schumacher 1973). Surely, he is one of the ultimate models of commitment to one's fellow man in the twentieth century. Both Gandhi and Schumacher expressed thoughts similar to those of Robert Chambers in his *Rural Development: Putting the Last First* (Chambers 1983, 2–3, 288–89). The following are some of a number of common themes that are essential to participatory management of service organizations:

1. Regard artisans, small farmers, laborers, and even the unemployed as fellow professionals and set out to learn from them.

2. Accept fellow professionals from other cultures as equals from whom you can learn.

3. Recognize that people are more important than technology because it takes people to implement technology.

4. Know that individuals with whom you work will be there to carry on long after you leave.

5. Realize that innovative systems, equipment, and husbandry are important but they are only a means to an end.

6. Accept the fact that these steps can only be a means to the end of training leader-managers, technicians, and laborers who will apply these innovations after we are gone (see 2 and 4).

INVOLVE EMPLOYEES IN PARTICIPATORY MANAGEMENT

The concept of participatory management is not easy to define. It has been described as a technique whereby employees are empowered to make decisions regarding how things are accomplished in their part of the organization.

> "The logic of participatory management is that hourly employees are the closest to the problems—and to their possible solution. Involving employees in the decision-making process is a way of sharing responsibility to achieve success" (Williams 1994).

In participatory service organizations workers at all levels as well as customers are empowered to make decisions regarding how things are accomplished. This approach may be more time consuming, but it is certainly one that has a far more lasting influence on the impact a service organization makes.

DRUCKER'S "DO THE RIGHT THING"

Chambers refers to

> "the litanies of rural developers which include 'We must educate the farmers' and 'We must uplift the rural (or urban) poor.' These can be stood on their heads. Outsiders have first to learn from farmers and from the rural and urban poor (as well as local development workers.) But many outsiders are hindered from such learning in reverse by their educational attainment, urban status, or roles as bearers and dispensers of modern knowledge" (Chambers 1983, 188–89).

According to Walton, Deming said it another way,

> "How to improve quality and productivity? 'By everyone doing his best.' Five words—and it is *wrong*. That is not the right answer. You have to know what to do, *then* do your best. Sure we need everybody's best—everybody working together with a common aim. And knowing something about how to achieve it" (Walton 1986).

In the words of Peter Drucker, we must "concentrate on being effective," even if we may appear to be inefficient in striving for this goal.

THE CHAMBERS-SCHWEITZER QUANDARY

Is there any single answer to the Chambers's quandary, a way "How to put the last first, which has not been discovered?" An early-inspired leader-manager in Africa, Albert Schweitzer, pondered this same question of motivating people to make the extra effort.

"I am convinced that there is far more in (human beings) of idealist willpower than ever comes to the surface of the world. Just as the water of the streams we see is small in amount compared to that which flows underground, so the idealism which becomes visible is small in amount compared with what men and women bear locked in their hearts, unrealized or scarcely released. To unbind what is bound, to bring the underground waters to the surface: mankind is waiting and longing for such as can do that" (Schweitzer 1949, 94).

Our challenge in managing service organizations is to "unbind what is bound, to bring the underground waters to the surface." We must realize that the management process in our organizations needs to motivate everyone related to its operation. This includes those being helped as well as the helpers who should be inspired to adopt this process as their goal and work together to attain it.

APPROACHES TO PARTICIPATORY MANAGEMENT

TRAIN AND MOTIVATE THE STAFF

As the subject of this chapter is Participatory Management, we must come back to Ita Hartnett's definition, mentioned on page xvi of the Introduction. *"Management is doing what you want with what you've got."* Hodja's quandary about dealing with his friend's fourth friend with the same sense of dedication and service that he had shown to his childhood friend clarifies the challenge.

Among service organizations there are three kinds of bridge builders—the "what we've got" of the Hartnett equation:

1. Government organizations
2. Profit-making (proprietary) organizations
3. Private voluntary organizations

All three types have done good and bad work. It is not so much a matter of the three approaches, but how well they train and motivate their staff—and what kind of a leader-manager is at the top.

Organizations such as these vary according to their size. There can be small or large government agencies, small or large businesses, and small or large private voluntary organizations. They differ, as well, in their origin depending on whether they are indigenous or exogenous organizations. They also vary between being client-oriented, seeking to serve their clients' interest, or being directed toward changing the behavior of their customers regardless of whether or not the customers want to be changed. The last distinction is probably the most significant for leader-managers regardless of which type of organization they are managing. Clearly, the principle of participatory management should apply to all three types, both for employees and outside customers.

APPLY A "DO WITH" APPROACH

In analyzing the concept of linkage among extension, research, and training, Professor Niels Röling of Wageningen University in Holland refers to the urgency of assuring that our "needs orientation" be "client oriented," recognizing that intervening organizations "cannot solve the problems unless they know what the problems are." He identifies three approaches:

1. The DO TO strategy asks the question: "How do I get them where I want them?"

2. The DO FOR strategy asks the question: "How do I develop an offering that my target clients want?"

3. The DO WITH strategy starts with the question: "How do I help people achieve what they themselves want to achieve?" (Röling 1988, 145).

The "what we want" side of the "what we want with what we've got" equation might best be described as " participatory management." Among Deming, Chambers, and Röling, this requires that the customers and the staff at all levels be given a sense of ownership in the effort and be encouraged to decide what changes *they* want and how these should be implemented.

AVOID THE PITFALLS OF LARGE ORGANIZATIONS

The following are some of the factors that hinder participatory management in large service organizations:

1. The promotion system is based on seniority rather than dedication or productivity.

2. Larger organizations do not always have the option of selecting limited populations to serve.

3. There tends to be a rhythm of work among larger service organizations that hinders rapid program implementation and flexibility.

4. Initiative is often penalized rather than rewarded by senior staff in large organizations.

APPLY PARTICIPATORY CONCEPTS

Advocates of one of the three approaches to development—government, proprietary, or voluntary—often make the mistake of championing one approach over another. They fail to realize that it is not a matter of which type of organization is implementing the development. The real question is more a matter of the quality of service provided by an organization. Its client orientation is far more important than the approach that it applies.

Some of the finest development organizations in post-war Greece were government agencies. One of them, the Mechanical Cultivation Service of the Ministry of Agriculture, literally transformed the Greek landscape. They converted swampland into rice paddies, terraced badly eroded cropland with rolling and bench terraces, and helped farmers to level and irrigate their fields. Corresponding examples of outstanding proprietary organizations and successful voluntary organizations abound throughout the world.

By the same token, it would be possible to describe a multitude of organizations in all three categories that have been total failures. What made the difference? The answer rests in the term *participatory* as applied to both management *and* development. Managers of all three types will succeed to the degree that their leader-managers apply participatory concepts to cultivating quality of management and prosperity of spirit. The remainder of this book is devoted to discussing approaches through which organizations can successfully implement participatory systems to strengthen their operations.

A NEW VARIETY OF "PROFESSIONALISM"

MULTIPLY THE NEW PROFESSIONALS

Chambers wrote of the "reversals" required for a new professionalism in service organizations *to put the last first*:

> "Reversals require professionals who are explorers and multi-disciplinarians, those who ask again and again, who will benefit and who will lose from their choices and actions. New professionals who put the last first already exist; the hard question is how they can multiply" (Chambers 1983, 168).

Chambers's counterpart in the business world, W. Edwards Deming, expressed the same challenge:

> "The cause of the decline (in industrial productivity) is that management have walked off the job of management, striving instead for dividends and good performance on the price of the company's stock" (Walton 1986, xi).

Deming's comment might be paraphrased to read, "the failure of many service organizations is that managers spend too much time striving to enhance their reputation or that of their organizations rather than serving their clients."

GIVE CUSTOMERS A VOICE

Deming recognized that workers were the only people in a position to actually control the production process in industry. Participatory leader-managers must recognize that those seeking assistance, guidance, or training must have a voice in the management and evaluation of their organizations as associates of the professionals with whom they are working. Without this participation, the organization is condemning itself to the same failures as its predecessors—outsiders sponsored by outsiders all of whom are convinced that they know better than those seeking help concerning how best to attain their goals.

APPLY FACILITATOR TECHNIQUES

Leader-managers of service organizations should apply quality techniques from industry and commerce. A key aspect of both philosophies is expressed by the term *empowerment*. They both distinguish among three kinds of leader-managers:

1. The first delegates tasks (responsibilities) to subordinates or local leaders, but retains authority over implementation.
2. The second delegates both the authority and the responsibility to implement delegated tasks. (In both situations, subordinates and local leaders are empowered to focus on problems, identify solutions, and implement them.)

3. The third, who has been referred to as a "facilitator-leader" by Arlen Etling (1994), studies a situation, decides what style of leadership is needed by the group, and acts accordingly.

According to Etling, facilitator leader-managers are capable of evaluating situations and individuals and applying appropriate techniques whether they are authoritarian, democratic, or laissez-faire. This requires a close participatory relationship with associates, having a feel of the pulse of the organization. Employee and local leader involvement requires that individuals, regardless of position, be included in the decision-making process. Through this approach the quality of relationships is enhanced. The message to staff and customers alike is that leader-managers have full confidence in their associates at all levels.

Valuing creativity, innovation, and respecting contrary ideas are additional precepts held by capable leader-managers. At the heart of Deming's, Chambers's, and Etling's philosophies is the need for tearing down the multitude of barriers which inhibit the flow of creativity and innovation—an essential attribute required of successful leader-managers.

In 1988, Tom Peters, in his book *Thriving on Chaos: Handbook for a Management Revolution*, wrote "the chief reason for [American industry's] failure in world-class competition is [its] failure to tap [the] work force's potential" (Peters 1988, 286). How easily one might transpose his statement and say that the "chief reason for the failure of many service organizations is their unwillingness to tap the potential of local professional and volunteer leadership, or of the urban and rural resource-poor laborers and farmers."

CONTINUALLY RETRAIN MANAGEMENT

Leader-manager skills development ties in closely with participatory management training. Deming frequently emphasized the process aspect of management as opposed to its structure. Vital to this process is the continual retraining of management. Dynamic, rejuvenating organizations that are determined to produce high-quality service provide ongoing opportunities for their managers and leaders to sharpen their leadership skills. Negative cultural and societal influences such as autocratic styles tend to intimidate workers and cultivate strained relationships between customers and management. These in turn breed a climate of fear—fear of change, fear of experimentation, fear of speaking up, and fear of being wrong. It is these same influences in large organizations that lead to jading among the staff. They create a constant climate of frustration among innovative and dynamic individuals at all levels, which eventually drives them to succumb to apathy.

IMPROVE THE WORK PROCESS

The primary goal of training in any organization must be to motivate all those associated with its efforts to improve the work process from the very bottom to the top. This applies equally to everyone from professionals and volunteers within the organization to the customers seeking some type of service. Newly acquired skills and attitudes must not be thought of as part of an abstract theoretical course. They must be directly applied as part of the trainees' daily activities and challenge—within the context of their working lives.

USE THE POLKA AS A TOOL

How can an organization maintain a participatory format under the pressures of daily challenges which so overwhelm its top managers? Possibly by following the formula discovered by the Greek dairy farmers described at the beginning of this chapter—"POLKA! POLKA!" The chapters which follow may help leader-managers think through how they might improve 1) the *planning* process, 2) the *organizational* structure, 3) *leadership* development, 4) quality centered *control*, and 5) provision for *adjustment* and flexibility.

These factors, applied cooperatively by leader-managers throughout any organization, will significantly contribute to the flavor of Hodja's "soup of the soup of the soup of the soup!"

TABLE 3.1 Self-Evaluation Form

CHAPTER 3: APPLY PARTICIPATORY TECHNIQUES Where are you as a leader-manager on the scale: *Kakomiris* (1) . . . to . . . *Nikokiris* (5)?						
TOPIC	1	2	3	4	5	PRIORITY
1. Assures vision percolates (page 23)						
2. Applies POLKA acronym (page 23)						
3. Always identifies "onebody" (page 26)						
4. Involves employees (page 27)						
5. Emphasizes *do the right thing* (page 27)						
6. Trains, motivates staff (page 28)						
7. Applies "do with" approach (page 28)						
8. Uses participatory concept (page 29)						
9. Gives customers a voice (page 30)						
10. Uses facilitator techniques (page 30)						
11. Retrains Management (page 31)						
12. Improves the work process (page 31)						

(Numbers in parentheses refer to pages where subject is mentioned.)

1. For each topic, place an "X" under the 1, 2, 3, 4, or 5 to show where you think you are now as a leader-manager.
2. For each topic, place a "Y" under the 1, 2, 3, 4, or 5 to show where you would like to be.
3. Mark any item where the topic does not apply to your program "NA" (Not Applicable).
4. Under priority, enter a number on a scale from 5 (top priority) to 1 (lowest priority).
5. Identify three or four of your primary concerns on this theme and develop a "POLKA" plan of work to deal with them.
6. List other concerns, share them with your associates, and evaluate them as above.

4

USE PLANNING AS A PARTICIPATORY TOOL

■ Can leader-managers assure participatory planning in contrast to top-down planning?

■ How can leader-managers generate confidence among associates or customers who lack training?

■ What is the distinction between telling some associates "why" and others "how?"

"It's me, Hodja, if God is willing."

Hodja was determined to be decisive and efficient. One day he told his wife he would plow his largest field on the far side of the river and be back for a big dinner. Say, "If Allah is willing," she urged him. He told her whether Allah was willing or not, that was his plan. The frightened wife looked up to Allah and asked forgiveness. Hodja loaded his wooden plow, hitched up the oxen to the wagon, climbed on his donkey, and set off. But within the short span of a day the river flooded from a cloudburst and washed his donkey downstream, and one of the oxen broke a leg in the mud, leaving Hodja to hitch himself in its place to plow the field. Having finished only half the field, at sunset he set out for home exhausted and soaking wet. The river was still high so he had to wait until long past dark to cross over. After midnight a very wet but much wiser Hodja knocked at his door. "Who is there?" asked his wife. "I think it is me, Hodja," he replied, "if Allah is willing!"

INTEGRATE PLANNING

Planning, in the eyes of the resource-poor farmer or marginal urban dweller, is the process of "deciding today what we will do tomorrow." Some leader-managers and development workers insist that plans be implemented whether, in Hodja's words, "Allah is willing or not." Wise leader-managers discovered long ago that even the best plans often depend on factors beyond their control.

Effective *nikokiris* recognize that successful planning is only part of four additional steps that are discussed in Chapters 5 through 8:

1. Helping local leaders or individuals to organize materials, people, funding.
2. Establishing clear lines of leadership and responsibility.
3. Providing control to be sure that the plan is being implemented as anticipated.
4. Assuring that adequate provision is made for flexibility and adjustment.

It is not surprising that planning remains one of the weakest links in many organizations and particularly among individuals living below the poverty line. They often fail to recognize that successful plans must integrate the other four steps in the management process. It was often amusing to sit in a Greek village coffee shop as the villagers sipped ouzo (the local alcoholic beverage) and listen to them expressing increasingly dreamy visions of "future plans and dreams for our village." The more ouzo they consumed, the more grandiose the plans. Unfortunately, all that remained of the plans the next morning was a headache!

MAKE THE PLAN PARTICIPATORY

PLAN FIRST, OR IDENTIFY THE PROBLEM?

Government officials, development workers, and voluntary organizations often come into communities with a "plan" long before the local citizens have even become aware of the problem. In other cases they appear with a problem identification quite different from any that the local community has observed. They end up looking like the three Boy Scouts who expeditiously move an elderly woman across a busy intersection, never realizing that she was waiting on that particular corner for a friend.

As in the story of Hodja's determination to plow up his field, those of us involved in development must ask:

1. Is our intervention needed?
2. Is the plan feasible?
3. Are we equipped to deal effectively with the plan?

Like Hodja we must learn to say "If Allah is willing!" from time to time.

LONG-TERM PLANNING ("STRATEGIC" IF YOU MUST!)

Planning is an ongoing process rather than an attainable objective, requiring continual review and re-evaluation. There is probably no single concept so commonly used by development workers and economists that intimidates local development workers and community leaders more than the term *strategic planning*! The concept originates from the same root as the Greek word *stratigos*, the rank of an army general. A "general's strategic plans" have little meaning and are thoroughly intimidating to army corporals or sergeants. This term is daunting to community leaders and local-level development workers. Strategic planning is a term which should be reserved for the "scientists" when they "speak about" their customers rather than when they "speak with" or "speak to" them.

THE ESSENCE OF PARTICIPATORY PLANNING

It is essential, in participatory planning, that the customers of an organization be involved in the planning from the early stages. Appendix 2 presents three case studies describing the involvement of the American Farm School in three unrelated aspects of planning over almost four decades beginning in 1958. The general principles, which were followed in each case, are summarized below. However, it will be of interest for anyone involved in the planning process to study the three cases. In all three, it became obvious that the plans could never have succeeded if they had not involved the customers in the decision-making process.

PLANNING BY COMMUNITY DEVELOPMENT—CASE STUDY I

COMMUNITY-WIDE PLANNING

The first case study describes a Community Development Program in the Prefecture (County) of Thessaloniki working with 151 villages. The program was initiated in 1958 with a grant of C$10,000 from the Unitarian Service Committee of Canada. It came to an unfortunate end in 1967 when the country was taken over by a dictatorial junta that had little confidence in democratic approaches to participatory development.

The goal of the program was to demonstrate three basic concepts of community development:

1. That members of a community could be *inspired to plan* their own future with minimum guidance from outside, once they established adequate communication amongst themselves.

2. That government agencies and other outsiders could be of help if *they saw their role as advisory.*

3. That communities could *implement their plans* once they had established an adequate system of communication within the community and with outsiders.

IMPROVING ORGANIZATIONAL PLANNING—CASE STUDY II

The second case study involved the American Farm School itself during a particularly turbulent period in its history between 1974 and 1978. The problems grew out of a growing lack of confidence in the management of the School among some of the Board of Trustees in the United States as well as disillusionment among many members of the staff.

There was a clear failure on my part as Director to communicate adequately, both with the Board and the staff. This upheaval took place during a period of strong anti-American sentiment in Greece following the seven-year junta. At the same time there were significant changes in Greek legislation which necessitated radical changes in the curriculum and the age level of the students. A series of steps were taken to clarify the School's mission and obtain agreement on the part of those involved in the programs. The Board and the administration determined that the following steps would best accomplish this goal:

1. Committees of the Board and the staff were appointed to clarify the School's Mission Statement.

2. Irwin Sanders, a consultant with a strong Greek background, was appointed to undertake a participatory survey involving Trustees, staff, students, and alumni.

3. With his help, the staff prepared a staging plan. They recognized that all the changes could not be accomplished at one time, but required agreement in a rational order.

4. Agreement was reached on a series of steps that would improve communications between all levels of the organization, particularly when new plans were implemented.

CROSS-CULTURAL "DO WITH" PLANNING

The third case study describes a rather innovative approach to the introduction of new systems of agricultural education in Albania. These programs included secondary agricultural education, adult education through short courses, and training programs in education at the Agricultural University at Tirana.

1. Albanian officials first identified that there was a clear "felt need" for practical secondary agricultural education and for teacher training in this field. This sentiment was shared by the Albanian Ministries of Education (MOE) and Agriculture (MOAF), the agricultural faculty of the Agricultural University of Tirana (AUT), as well as the Directors at the Schools and the agricultural faculty.

2. The existence of the American Farm School, a few hours drive from the Greek-Albanian border, provided a prototype of what the Albanian counterparts were seeking to create.

3. Recent Greek and American retirees from the Farm School as well as other specialists were available to conduct seminars and act as consultants in program implementation.

4. There was both the dedication and the capacity on the part of the Albanian counterparts involved, from the Ministerial and Rector level to the directors and staff of the schools, to assure the implementation of the program described in Appendix 2.

5. This was clearly an Albanian project supported by a number of foreign groups rather than a project imposed on the Albanian people by a group of foreigners.

IDENTIFY KEY STEPS IN PLANNING

The period of turbulence at the American Farm School in the 1970s prompted the administration to review its own planning process. The various elements identified at that time proved to be a useful guide for the Albanian schools. They have also proved most helpful in preparing workbooks for voluntary organizations in a number of countries as diverse as Nepal, Nigeria, Honduras, Bulgaria, and the United States. Just as with other elements of the management process, specific activities are not isolated. They are an integral part of a continuum. Planning reflects a process that may look ahead for as much as ten years while including hourly, daily, and weekly plans for a variety of individuals and departments in an organization.

FIVE-YEAR BROAD-BRUSH SKETCH

Larger organizations find it helpful to look ahead for a ten-year period. The Sanders report for the American Farm School in the 1970s contributed to two dimensions of the planning process. The first was comprised of ten specific recommendations, each of which required approval by the Board of Trustees. Twenty years later, a similar set of recommendations provided the basis for the three-way agreement among the Albanian MOE, MOAF, and AUT for the reorganization of agricultural schools.

The second part of the Sanders study outlined a plan for the institution which was not so concerned with exact implementation dates for specific projects as much as with broad-brush sketches of programs and the installations at the end of the decade. This approach had enabled the administration to envisage plant facilities, personnel, and budgetary requirements for the years ahead and to submit a five-year plan for consideration by the Board.

PLAN BY BUDGETING

The medium-term planning at the American Farm School is best reflected in a five-year budget. The section for the first year is highly detailed; that for the second outlines the programs that the School expects to implement. The sections for the third, fourth, and fifth years are much more broadly based but still stand up to close scrutiny.

A flow chart of a five-year plan, based on Dr. Sanders's recommendations and a five-year budget based on this plan, were submitted to the Board of Trustees. Each year since these were compiled, the staff has reviewed the previous year's accomplishments, updated those for the subsequent years, and worked on projections for the final year. The discipline of coordinating program and budget planning has been most useful to everyone concerned and played an invaluable role in the management process.

MBO AS A PLANNING TOOL

Probably no management concept was more generally accepted by industry in the second half of the twentieth century than management by objectives (MBO). Peter Drucker, the sage among managers, sees the role of the MBO approach as follows:

> "Management is not just a creature of the economy; it is a creator as well. And only to the extent to which it masters the economic circumstances, and alters them by conscious, directed action, does it really manage. To manage a business (or an organization) means, therefore, to *manage by objectives*" (Drucker 1968, 23–24).

Each member of the hierarchy must think of himself or herself as a creator of the process, not just a creation of it.

CLARIFY OBJECTIVES

The Farm School endeavored to implement this system by having department heads prepare their annual objectives after reviewing those of the heads of divisions, which are in turn based on the objectives of the associate director and the director.

Objectives should include:

1. definition of the objective
2. responsibility for implementation
3. date of completion
4. budget provisions
5. outside support

Implied in the concept of management by objectives is self-control. Managers are expected to inform their supervisors when they are not meeting their objectives. At the same time, however, associate directors are responsible for ensuring that each of their departments is meeting its objectives. Deming and other TQM "wise men" have expressed some reservations about MBO. In Hodja's words, "MBO is right, and TQM is right too" (see Hodja story beginning of Chapter 6). Instead of saying as Hodja's wife did, "They can't both be right!" the wise manager will climb on his donkey (riding backward) and discover that there are significant elements of both philosophies which can contribute to effective planning in their organization.

DAILY PLAN OF OBJECTIVES

Both over-optimism and an inclination to avoid unpleasant tasks hinder effective short-term planning in most institutions. A stream of unscheduled visitors requiring time and attention constantly interrupts Farm School staff members and their plan of work. Certain techniques have been helpful in overcoming these problems. An effective device for day-to-day planning is the 3" x 5" card used in libraries, as evidenced in the following story.

> The story was told to a Farm School administrator of a man who made a proposal to the president of a big steel company. He requested half an hour for consultation from each of the ten top executives. He stipulated that he wanted no payment unless the efficiency of the company had increased sufficiently at the end of the year to warrant a $25,000 fee. A year later he received the bank check. His proposal had been quite simple. He had asked each executive to make a list every morning on a 3" x 5" card, similar to those used in library reference trays, of the five most important jobs for that day. Regardless of what else they did, they committed themselves to accomplishing the items listed on the card.

This approach was introduced to the top staff at the Farm School, who accepted it with reservations. Only by observing the increased effectiveness of the managers who did adopt the system were the others convinced of its value. Over the years, the 3" x 5" card has become a mark of an effective manager, although some use variations of the same principle. The staff members have identified three main advantages to this system:

1. The card is readily available to write down an idea.
2. It commits the user in writing to dealing with his problems.
3. It provides a means of self-evaluation at the end of each day.

Objections have been raised in a number of countries where paper was scarce and no 3" x 5" cards were available. Folding a sheet of A4 or 8 1/2" x 11" paper three times provides thirty-two equivalents to the card, and also a useful record of a month's accomplishments.

MONTHLY AND ANNUAL CALENDARS

To ensure effective communication, the school circulates a monthly as well as an annual calendar. The monthly calendars indicate dates and times for activities such as Board meetings, staff meetings, short-course programs, and daily schedules. To prepare these calendars, each department must anticipate its schedule of activities for the year and participate in joint planning and coordination among the departments. These schedules tie in closely with the statement of the overall objectives of the school's two main divisions: education and the model farm. They provide everyone in the institution with a clear understanding of the goals for the year and plans for their implementation. By looking at these calendars, each staff member involved in a variety of activities is aware of the previous commitments of other staff members. "Avoid surprises" is wise counsel for any institutional administrator.

Although the description of short-term planning at the Farm School indicates that the institution is very efficient and effective, this has not always been the case. However, the guidelines do exist and constant effort is made to encourage everyone to use the 3" x 5" cards, pocket diaries, and the annual calendar. The staff members have learned over the years how important flexibility is in planning. When they were originally asked to prepare one-year plans, the usual reaction was, "How do I know what will be happening in six months' time?" They have found, however, that it is

Better to plan and even plan wrong than not to plan at all.

"MAKE NO LITTLE PLANS"

Thirty-five years ago, it seemed doubtful to most Greek people that either urban or rural residents, or the civil servants assigned to help them, would be able to make long-term plans for their small businesses, their lives, or their communities. Growing numbers of these individuals have learned to plan and, as a result, development workers have become better able to help them in their planning. Surely this progress must inspire local citizens and their leaders, as well as civil servants elsewhere, to follow in their footsteps.

The following quotation was given to me by Ruth Wells, a trustee of the American Farm School, whose husband, George, President and CEO of the American Optical Company, was a descendant of Daniel H. Burnham, a nineteenth-century architect.

"Make no little plans," said Burnham, "for they have no magic to stir men's blood and probably themselves will not be realized. Make big plans, aim high in hope and work, remembering that a noble, logical diagram once recorded will never die, but long after we are gone will be a living thing, asserting itself with ever-growing insistence" (Burnham 1970).

"STRUCTURE BECOMES POETRY, ENGINEERING BECOMES ART"

A major element in Burnham's "big plans" reflects a capacity on the part of certain organizations to reach out beyond program-oriented plans and goals. Another architect, Richard Swibold, expressed this concept through his profession:

> "Most of us usually see only the concrete and glass, but occasionally, the hands and heads of the makers join together—structure becomes poetry, engineering becomes art" (quoted to the author by Swibold's daughter, Katherine).

Development plans in which "structure becomes poetry and engineering becomes art" must reflect goals which bring happiness, warmth, and joy into the lives of those with whom we are working, even though they may be living in a state of abject poverty. Such goals are reflected in friendly smiles of acceptance, kind words of encouragement, a sincere note of appreciation. Returning to Deming, it is not enough for such goals to be the possession of top management in the organization.

WHEN PROFESSIONALS, VOLUNTEERS, AND CUSTOMERS THINK TOGETHER

"Why is it that non governmental organizations (NGOs) which know less of the science of development are better in their application than the government agencies?" asked Stanley Khaila, Director of the Social Science Research Institute in Malawi. It may well be because in the more dynamic NGOs the hands and heads of the makers have joined together, their structure has become poetry and their engineering has become art!

It is when these dimensions are continually cultivated in the planning of the development process that the professionals are able to avoid becoming jaded and look on each new day as being "a day the Lord hath made!" Whatever task they undertake, they will feel confident that it will be accomplished with an ease and efficiency inspired by such convictions percolating throughout their organization.

IDENTIFY QUALITY OF SPIRIT IN ORGANIZATIONS

During a period of ten years following our retirement from the American Farm School, my wife and I have been privileged to visit a variety of organizations in a number of developing nations. In many different countries, Tad and I were particularly impressed by the diversity of "quality of spirit" between otherwise similar programs.

Chapters 9 and 10 attempt to identify the particular attributes among inspired and inspiring leader-managers which contribute to the spirit. We noticed it in agricultural schools in Albania, Tanzania, and Nigeria, in post-secondary schools in Malawi and the Dominican Republic, and in development organizations in Nepal and Honduras, as we had in a variety of institutions in Greece over the years.

INCORPORATE "WHY" IN THE PLANNING PROCESS

A new spirit in the planning process has brought a major change, which recognizes the hunger of human souls, to be validated as worthwhile individuals. As Charles Coonradt said:

> "To important people we tell 'why,' and to unimportant people we simply tell 'how.' People can tell how you feel about them by whether you tell them why or how" (Coonradt 1984).

It is not enough to have plans that tell people how. Service organizations led by inspiring leader-managers become art and poetry when they incorporate the concept of *why* among all those involved in the process of their participatory planning.

TURNING DREAMS INTO REALITIES

Most human beings through the ages anticipated little more for their offspring than that which they had themselves. But some *nikokiris* had higher aspirations for their children and their grandchildren. The success of their dreams was assured because they were based on plans that would turn them into reality and were prepared in consultation with the new generation. The *kakomiris*, the loser, either had no plans at all for his children or was inclined to formulate unrealistic plans. The *nikokiris* included specific objectives with time frames, clarified responsibilities, estimated costs, and anticipated results.

IF ALLAH IS WILLING

Marginal farmers are at a serious disadvantage compared to their urban brothers who are able to close the shutter on their store or the door to their office at night. The latter need not worry about weather or other such factors beyond their control. No matter how carefully the peasant or marginal inner-city resident plans, however, he still must say, like Hodja, "This is my plan. I think it will succeed, if Allah is willing." The *nikokiris*, among urban and rural dwellers alike, are the ones who make use of every available resource to ensure that within their personal abilities and limitations, their plans will succeed—*if Allah is willing!*

TABLE 4.1 Self-Evaluation Form

CHAPTER 4: USE PLANNING AS A PARTICIPATORY TOOL						
Where are you as a leader-manager on the scale: *Kakomiris* (1) . . . to . . . *Nikokiris* (5)?						
TOPIC	**1**	**2**	**3**	**4**	**5**	**PRIORITY**
1. Uses participatory planning (page 37)						
2. Applies five-year planning (page 40)						
3. Applies one-year planning (page 40)						
4. Plans by budgeting (page 40)						
5. Uses MBO as tool (page 40)						
6. Clarifies objectives (page 41)						
7. Uses organizational monthly calendar (page 42)						
8. Uses daily 3" x 5" card concept (page 41)						
9. "Makes big plans" (page 42)						
10. Joins professionals, volunteers, and customers in planning (page 43)						
11. Incorporates "why" in plans (page 44)						
12. Turns dreams into realities (page 44)						

(Numbers in parentheses refer to pages where subject is mentioned.)

1. For each topic, place an "X" under the 1, 2, 3, 4, or 5 to show where you think you are now as a leader-manager.
2. For each topic, place a "Y" under the 1, 2, 3, 4, or 5 to show where you would like to be.
3. Mark any item where the topic does not apply to your program "NA" (Not Applicable).
4. Under priority, enter a number on a scale from 5 (top priority) to 1 (lowest priority).
5. Identify three or four of your primary concerns on this theme and develop a "POLKA" plan of work to deal with them.
6. List other concerns, share them with your associates, and evaluate them as above.

DECIDE WHO SHOULD ORGANIZE

- What do we mean by Structure and Process in organizing?

- How do we move from Structure to Process?

- What are the cultural changes in an organization as it moves from Structure to Process?

"It's in your hands."

One day two small boys decided to play a trick on Hodja. With a tiny bird cupped in their hands they would ask him whether it was alive or dead. If he said it was alive they would crush it to show him he was wrong. If he said it was dead they would let it fly away and still fool him. When they found the wise old man they said, "Hodja, that which we are holding, is it alive or dead?" Hodja thought for a moment and replied, "Ah, my young friends, that is in your hands."

STRUCTURE AND PROCESS IN ORGANIZATION

This chapter analyzes the four key ingredients of organizing. The two major components are *structure*, the skeletal dimension, and *process*, the way in which the structural elements relate to each other. There is, furthermore, a *historical* aspect to organization, reflecting the relationship of structure and process over a period of time. Finally, there is an *ethereal* dimension to organization that is identified as "quality."

IN WHOSE HANDS?

Organizing is a procedure used by leader-managers to coordinate the factors of production—people, equipment, supplies, savings, credit, and property—to assist the *nikokiris* in management. Leader-managers, employees at every level, and volunteers must recognize that successful organizing is "in their hands." A shrewd Greek stone mason, Mastro Christo, expressed this concept in his own terms:

> "It isn't enough to know how to build walls. We must know how to organize our work and relate to our employees and our customers. It's in our hands!"

STRUCTURE VS. PROCESS

Mastro Christo's view applies equally to building walls as well as to forming and managing organizations. *Nikokiris* organizations reflect procedures that generate continuous improvement, permeating the very fabric of the organization. Most people think of organization as the procedure used to establish *structure*. When traditional managers or consultants comment "That's a poorly organized operation," they are usually berating the absence of adequate structure in the organization.

Leader-managers recognize *process* as an equally important ingredient, assuring the organization's capacity to adapt to changing circumstances required to meet customer needs. Some organizations tend to be overly structure-oriented. Emphasis on structure supports rigid, authoritarian management. Process-oriented organizations are more flexible, more dependent on human interrelationships among the staff, and also more customer-oriented. The older and the larger an organization, the greater its tendency toward structure orientation.

ZEN AND THE ART OF ORGANIZATION

The book, *Zen and the Art of Motorcycle Maintenance* (Pirsig 1979), should be required reading for all students of management. The central character of the book describes his total, uncalculating attachment to his motorcycle. He distinguishes between two components to describe his machine. *Structure* is used to point out each of the basic parts—frame, wheels, engine, handlebars, power chain, and tires. In contrast he speaks of the *function (process)* which describes the role of each of the parts, how they operate, and their relationship to each other. The structure and function metaphor of a motorcycle is similar to the two key components for organizing a service organization. Soon after the book was published, we introduced the largest, flashiest motorcycle we could borrow for the annual staff conference at the American Farm School. It proved to be a memorable visual aid.

STRUCTURE IN ORGANIZATIONS

ORGANIZATIONAL GUIDELINES

The American Farm School's experience over ninety years proves to be a useful guide for leader-managers of service organizations. The School's administrative chart in the 1980s (Figure 5.1) will help the reader understand its structure at that time. The chart was prepared to define the working relationships among the staff to ensure that everyone was making a maximum contribution toward the objectives of the School. It also clarified a unity of command through which final authority was delegated to one individual in each department or division. Department heads, as leader-managers, were encouraged to delegate their authority to assure more effective management.

ORDERLINESS

Orderliness is one of the most obvious indicators of effective organization. Equipment properly stored, well-maintained buildings, neat landscaping, and well-kept gardens reflect a *nikokiris* organization. A *nikokiris* leader-manager and staff within such organizations make good use of their time, assure maximum use of facilities, and prepare well-organized plans of work. Capital and operating budgets, inventories, replacement programs, credit planning, and marketing plans are indicative of orderly procedures.

Each of the employees looking upon themselves as leader-managers must feel a part of the organization, developing a sense of responsibility for activities assigned to them. Plans must be periodically assessed to ensure that all aspects of the organization's work are integrated, assuring adequate horizontal and vertical communication. However, organization has little value if it is not primarily directed to serving an agency's clients.

WHO HAS THE AUTHORITY?

Who has the authority to establish the procedures that assure orderliness? Who will have the authority to assure the implementation of these procedures once they are established? At the Farm School these tasks were traditionally assigned to the business manager, personnel director, and the finance director. They organized the systems and were responsible for their implementation. Was this enough? Obviously the ultimate responsibility had to rest with top management. As President Harry Truman took delight in pointing out, "The buck stops here!" (Responsibility ultimately rests with the top person.) It became increasingly obvious as the School grew and the staff increased that something more was needed. Both management and the staff began to realize that the organization could not hope to operate effectively until authority was delegated through all levels of the operation.

FLEXIBLE GUIDE

As authority is delegated throughout an organization, the management system becomes a process while the organizational chart becomes a guide. The function of the chart is to help guide the staff as it strives toward an agreed-upon goal. In order for this new approach to succeed, the number of employees that reports to any one supervisor should be limited to assure maximum communication. Although this number depends on the ability of the workers, the activities of a department, and the geographical area covered by the program, no one person should have more than six to eight individuals directly respon-

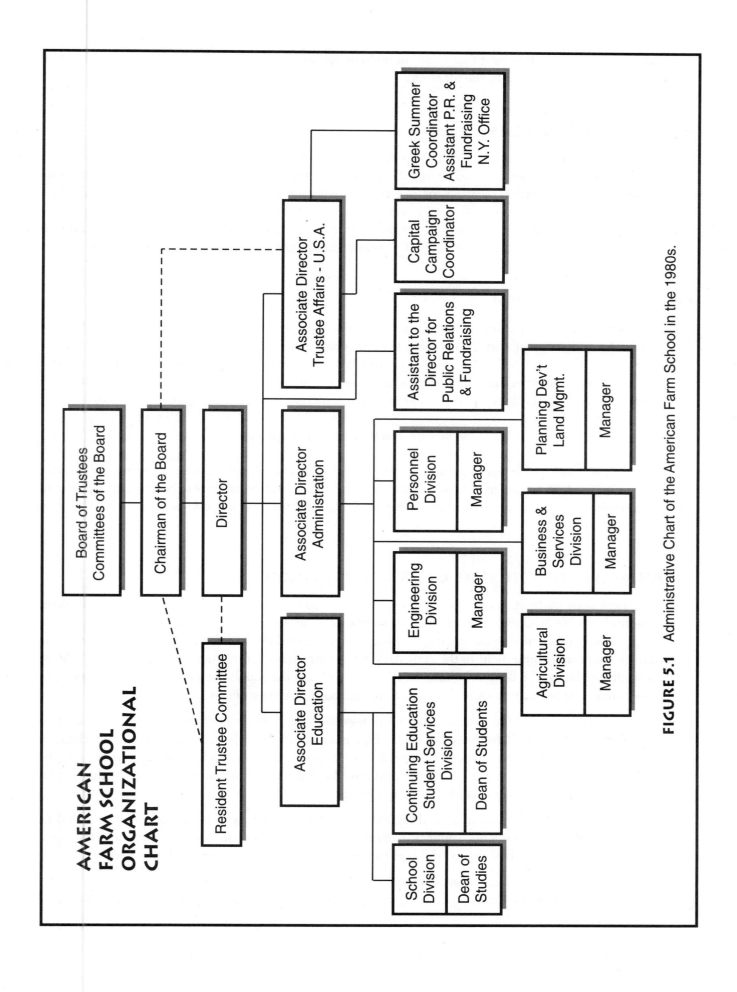

AMERICAN FARM SCHOOL ORGANIZATIONAL CHART

Board of Trustees
Committees of the Board

Chairman of the Board

Director

Resident Trustee Committee

Associate Director
Trustee Affairs - U.S.A.

Greek Summer Coordinator
Assistant P.R. &
Fundraising
N.Y. Office

Capital
Campaign
Coordinator

Assistant to the
Director for
Public Relations
& Fundraising

Associate Director
Administration

Personnel
Division

Manager

Engineering
Division

Manager

Planning Dev't
Land Mgmt.

Manager

Business &
Services
Division

Manager

Agricultural
Division

Manager

Associate Director
Education

Continuing Education
Student Services
Division

Dean of Students

School
Division

Dean of
Studies

FIGURE 5.1   Administrative Chart of the American Farm School in the 1980s.

sible to him or her. It is vital that these individuals operate as a team with each other as well as with their immediate superior in the hierarchy.

ROLE OF VOLUNTEERS

Closely linked to the interrelationships among personnel is the cooperation required among volunteer workers, trustees (where they exist), trainees, and staff. Programs in which trainees, students or other customers are involved in decision-making are invariably more successful. As lower level leader-managers, technicians and laborers should also have a voice in organizing their own department. Even though volunteers should be allowed to make suggestions to management, they should be discouraged from interfering with the internal lines of communication indicated in the organization chart.

ONE MAN, ONE BOSS!

No matter how much team spirit is cultivated among the staff, there must always be clear lines of authority and responsibility. A top management consultant in Greece, Nicholas Ebeoglou, often referred to a Greek proverb—"Every dog should know his own boss, and every boss his dog." At a management seminar at the School, a number of staff members tried to point out specific exceptions in which an individual might report to more than one superior. Ebeoglou categorically replied,

"One man, one boss! One man, one boss!"

This phrase has become legendary at the Farm School since Ebeoglou conducted a seminar for the staff in the 1970s. A personnel manual which states the rights and responsibilities of both the employee and the employer as well as a job description defining relationships to others is vital to avoid confusion in this area.

WEAKNESSES IN THE STRUCTURAL APPROACH

Inexperienced leader-managers become overly dependent on administrative charts for their authority. These charts institutionalize the chain of command and can stand in the way of a more flexible process approach. It takes new leader-managers time to overcome their dependence on the rigidity of the boxes—especially their own! In the early days of the Farm School, the often-heard expression "We are a family" reflected the flexible communicative spirit among the staff. When less secure managers take over, they tend to become more dependent on rigid administrative charts.

An even more serious indication of the weakness of these charts was expressed by their failure to mention students, adult trainees, contributors, customers of the School farm, or the approximately 10,000 visitors who came to the School each year. It appeared as if this entire group was outside the School's structure. How much better it would have been if a new line had been added to the bottom which would have appeared as illustrated in Figure 5.2.

Furthermore, if this chart were to be designed in the spirit of participatory development, it would be turned upside down. Students, trainees, customers, employees, contributors, campers, and their parents would be at the top of the pyramid where they would command the attention they deserve.

A third major shortcoming of organizational charts is the absence of horizontal lines to assure interdepartmental communication and problem-solving at all levels. The charts look like an animal with four

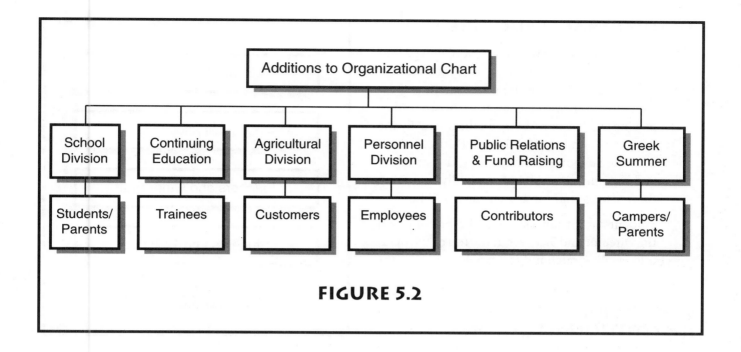

FIGURE 5.2

legs with each leg operating independently of the others. This is not unlike Hodja's proverbial camel, which he described as *a horse designed by a committee*. All the members have a tendency to talk at the same time while nobody is listening!

HISTORICAL FRAMEWORK

No organizational chart can exist independently. It usually has a past, a flexible present, and a future. The chart in Figure 5.1 reflects the "present" of the 1980s. What the School looked like seventy years earlier, a few years after it was founded, is illustrated in Figure 5.3.

PROCESS-ORIENTED BEGINNINGS

When John Henry House founded the American Farm School, he and his wife, Adeline, thought of themselves and their School as true servants of the students and adult trainees whom they taught. The members of the Board of Trustees were organized in the United States to assist him by raising funds for the School, and saw themselves as helpers. Based on this interpretation, one might say that the 1904 conceptual organizational chart would have looked something like Figure 5.3. Students and trainees were at the top, and the Director and Trustees at the bottom of the pyramid.

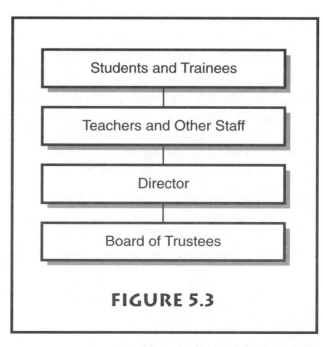

FIGURE 5.3

TRADITIONAL STRUCTURE

With the passage of time the School moved into a more traditional structure as it received formal recognition from the government and established itself with a charter of incorporation placing legal responsibility on the Board. By the time the founder, John Henry House, turned over the School to his successor, the structure had become inverted. It was rapidly becoming the Trustees' and top management's School.

Students and trainees are at the bottom, and the Director and Trustees at the top of the pyramid, as illustrated in Figure 5.4.

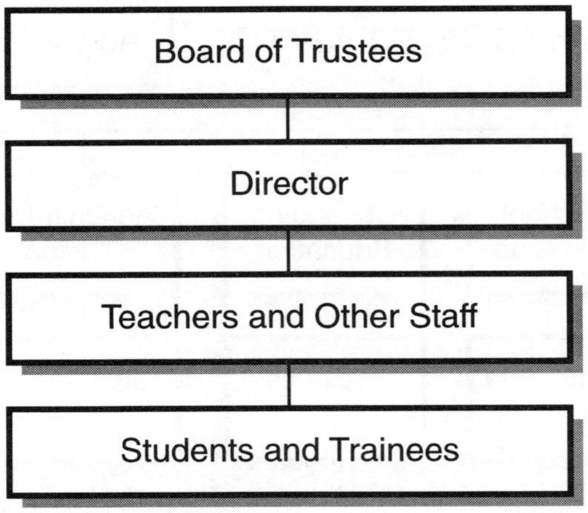

STRUCTURAL INSTITUTIONALIZATION

In time, a new "top-down" structure had become well established. Institutionalization took over, with structure in the dominant position over process. It came as no surprise that seventy years after the School was founded, the staff organized a union to protect their rights and defend the tradition of the School (as they saw it). Even less surprising was the student strike a few years later through which the students sought to demand their share of the authority in the management of the School. It appears that neither staff nor students felt that the School was serving their best interests in their roles as customers.

TURN STRUCTURES UPSIDE DOWN

Few managers and trustees would accept the idea of turning the organizational chart in Figure 5.1 upside down, back to the John Henry House tradition of Figure 5.3. No doubt both employees and customers would misinterpret a chart such as this. However, there are a number of steps which could be implemented in the leader-manager framework to give internal (employees) and external customers (students, trainees, and contributors) the feeling that the entire organization is genuinely concerned about them and their problems.

Once the academic staff gave more authority to the Student Council, the students' perception of the faculty changed. It gave them a sense of a participatory approach on the part of management of student affairs. The students, a group of parents, and the faculty were able to prepare a new set of rules and regulations acceptable to students and faculty alike. It would have been far healthier for the School if the administration had taken the initiative to share authority with the students, something that could have been done earlier.

Board of Trustees

Director

Teachers and Other Staff

Students and Trainees

FIGURE 5.4

THE PROCESS OF ORGANIZATION

WHAT IS MEANT BY PROCESS?

What is meant by process as a major component of organization? Process is the operating procedure that affects the delicate interaction of people, machines, materials, and the environment. Among leader-managers in voluntary organizations and participatory development organizations, process is a customer-oriented procedure based on anticipating and even exceeding customer needs and expectations. The process of quality service is neither a goal nor an objective, but a way of implementing customer-oriented assistance and development. Such customer-driven organizations begin by developing approaches at all levels that listen to the customers.

IDENTIFY CUSTOMERS AS ORGANIZERS

Customer focus is probably the key ingredient of process, implemented by leader-managers, in voluntary organizations. Customers are not limited to those who buy or benefit from the products of an organization. They include the employees (who may also be suppliers), volunteers, as well as trustees or others responsible for supervision. It is the satisfaction of these individuals that the organization must seek to fulfill. They are the ones who define quality. The major challenge of any organization is to establish a system that assures continual communication with the customer. Obviously the key customer in the organizational process is the individual, neighborhood, community, or larger political entity receiving assistance. Neither staff nor trainees in service organizations should be overlooked in their role as customers.

FOCUS ON THE "POLITY FOR CAPACITY BUILDING"

How can leader-managers consult with their potential customers among the poor either in the inner cities of the West or in the developing world? In the minds of traditional managers the change is almost as revolutionary as turning the organizational chart upside down. James Gustave Speth, administrator of the United Nations Development Program, speaks of focusing "on the polity" (body politic, the people) rather than the economy for "capacity building." Is it possible to develop "capacity building" without the involvement of those whose capacity we seek to build?

THE CAUSE OF THE FAILURES

Most managers of assistance programs argue that neither they nor their clients have time for the luxury of such communication. The main cause of the failures over three decades, described in a *New York Times* article in April 1996 from Ougadougou, the capital of Burkina Faso in West Africa, was the lack of empowerment of the people. Aid agencies did not have time forty years ago to consult their clients, and are today paying the price. This shortcoming parallels the experiences of President Johnson's "Great Society" programs designed to solve many of the problems of the inner cities of the United States over thirty years. Surely we must take the time now to avoid similar failures in the coming three decades.

TABLE 5.1 Organization Cultural Changes From Structure Oriented to Participatory Process Organization

FROM	TO
Hierarchical style	Participatory style More horizontal organization
Top-down information flow	Top-down, lateral, and upward information
Inward focus on quality	Customer-defined quality
Functional focus	Process focus
Short-term planning	A vision for the future
Episodic improvements	Comprehensive and continuous improvements
Top-down initiatives	All staff involved and engaged
Manage	Delegate/Lead/Coach
Direct	Empower
Employees a cost	Employees an asset
Counsel	Ownership/Participation
Functional, narrow-scope jobs	Integrated functions, work teams
Enforcement from the top	Promoting mutual trust

Source: Alper Associates, 1992.

FUNDAMENTAL CULTURAL CHANGES

Table 5.1, from *Understanding the Basic Concepts of TQM*, provides a useful outline of fundamental cultural changes that must take place in substituting process for structure among participatory organizations. At the heart of this apparently drastic metamorphosis there must always lie two fundamental questions:

1. "Did our customers have a voice in the design of our product?"
2. "Did our customers, internal and external alike, wake up satisfied with the quality of our product today (Alper Associates 1992)?

IMPLICATIONS FOR INSPIRED LEADER-MANAGERS

TURNING EMPLOYEES INTO ORGANIZERS

Leader-managers, trustees, or other staff members must decide whether to start thinking seriously about adopting a Quality Management approach. Richard Williams's book, *Essentials of Total Quality Management* (TQM) (Williams 1994, 46–51), to which I have referred extensively, is particularly helpful. It is essential reading for those who wish for a better understanding of the philosophy of TQM. A clearer explanation of TQM tools, techniques, and training as well as management approaches will also be needed. Equally important is the identification of a competent TQM consultant who can guide the organization through the procedure. Organizations interested in implementing TQM should bear in mind that William Alper, a specialist in quality management in service organizations, speaks of a five-year implementation process.

QUALITY AND PARTICIPATORY DEVELOPMENT

Earlier discussions in this book of the parallel thinking of Deming and Chambers have referred to the close affinity of the two approaches in business and voluntary organizations. Both insist on incorporating all those who are a part of the development process as an integral part of the team. All levels from top management and trustees to lower level staff as well as those seeking help from the organizations should be included. They are all the ultimate customers of the process in the urban and rural areas of the world.

THE MALAWI EXAMPLE

The Malawi organization, Christian Service Committee (CSC), is an outstanding example of a service organization. It has successfully integrated paid staff, volunteers, government workers, and marginal landholders as members of a development team. In a very real sense CSC has integrated management principles based on its own participatory approach. As indigenous churches, they are helping marginalized communities and farm families in their own districts. They are exogenous to those seeking assistance, but are culturally more closely integrated. As Malawians they are less of a threat to the communities than exogenous workers from distant cities or foreign lands.

TRAINING LEADER-MANAGERS ABOUT PROCESS

Thousands of organizations in many countries have incorporated participatory management as an integral part of organizing their operations. Many have taken one step further and integrated it into their participatory development programs. Here they place major emphasis on training leader-managers. They have also placed greater emphasis on commitment to process. This commitment does not require replacing structure with process. It does recognize the importance of increasing emphasis on process over structure. It might be helpful to revert to the motorcycle metaphor to clarify the challenge.

MOTORCYCLES AND DEVELOPMENT

Early in his book, Robert Pirsig, the author of *Zen and the Art of Motorcycle Maintenance*, identifies two components of his motorcycle, structure and function (process) (page 49). Once he completes this analysis, however, he has a nervous breakdown. He is convinced that there is a third ingredient, even more important than either structure or function, which he cannot identify. After his release from a mental hospital, as he drives his young son across the country on his motorcycle, he has an inspiration. He identifies the lost ingredient as:

QUALITY!

THE ELUSIVE NATURE OF "QUALITY"

Despite several chapters devoted to explaining the concept, Pirsig can only define quality indirectly.

> "Care and Quality are internal and external aspects of the same thing. A person who sees Quality and feels it as he works is a person who cares" (Pirsig 1979, 218).

> "Quality cannot be defined. If we do define it, we are defining something less than quality itself" (Pirsig 1979, 251).

It comes as no surprise that a review of a number of books on quality management also failed to produce an adequate definition of quality. Pirsig finally concludes,

> "The real cycle you're working on is a cycle called yourself. The machine that appears to be 'out there' and the person that appears to be 'in here' are not two separate things. They grow toward Quality or fall away from Quality together" (Pirsig 1979, 325).

The people whom inspired leader-managers seek to help "out there" and the leader-managers' organizations "in here" are not two separate entities. They "grow toward Quality or fall away from Quality together." If leader-managers are to succeed as managers of service organizations, they should distinguish between structure and process in *their own* organizations. They need to help those with whom they work to distinguish between structure and process in *their own* work. They should never forget that in addition to these two components there is a third quality, referred to in this book as "Prosperity of Spirit." It is the discovery of this elusive dimension that will give final meaning to their efforts as organizers. Will they succeed? In the words of Hodja, "That, my friends, is in *your* hands!"

TABLE 5.2 Self-Evaluation Form

CHAPTER 5: DECIDE WHO SHOULD ORGANIZE						
Where are you as a leader-manager on the scale: *Kakomiris* (1) . . . to . . . *Nikokiris* (5)?						
TOPIC	1	2	3	4	5	PRIORITY
1. Hierarchical to participatory style						
2. Top-down info. Flow to lateral, upward						
3. Inward focus to customer quality						
4. Short-term plan to future vision						
5. Functional to process focus						
6. Episodic to continual improvements						
7. Top-down initiative to all staff						
8. Manage to delegate/lead/coach						
9. Direction to empowerment						
10. Employees a cost to an asset						
11. Top-down counsel to participation						
12. Functional, narrow scope jobs to integrated work teams						

(This self-evaluation is based on Table 5.1 on page 56.)

1. For each topic, place an "X" under the 1, 2, 3, 4, or 5 to show where you think you are now as a leader-manager.
2. For each topic, place a "Y" under the 1, 2, 3, 4, or 5 to show where you would like to be.
3. Mark any item where the topic does not apply to your program "NA" (Not Applicable).
4. Under priority, enter a number on a scale from 5 (top priority) to 1 (lowest priority).
5. Identify three or four of your primary concerns on this theme and develop a "POLKA" plan of work to deal with them.
6. List other concerns, share them with your associates, and evaluate them as above.

6

BECOME A LEADER-MANAGER

- What is meant by the term "leader-manager"?

- What are the languages used by leader-managers?

- Can leadership skills be enhanced among managers?

- What attributes must managers cultivate to become effective leader-managers?

"My donkey and I are compromising!"

For many years there has been a bronze casting at the Farm School of Hodja riding backward on a donkey. It relates to the time when he was seen in the village riding his beloved donkey backwards. When a neighbor asked him why he was facing that way Hodja said, "My friend here wanted to go one way and I wanted to go the other, so we are compromising."

WHO ARE THE LEADERS?

MANAGERS AS LEADERS

Many newly appointed managers have the idea when "in the saddle" they can comfortably settle in, assured that they now have full authority. They feel confident that they can decide in which direction their organization should move and how to proceed. They soon learn, like the wise Hodja, that nothing could be farther from the truth. As they discover the distinction between managers-as-leaders and leaders-as-managers, they are able to convert the science of management into the art of leadership and attain the status of leader-manager. By then they will have mastered the skill of riding a prized steed backward and sideways, as well as facing forward.

STATUS OF MANAGERS

The early Christians had a far better understanding of the status of an effective leader-manager:

> "You know that those who are recognized as rulers . . . lord it over them; and their great men exercise authority over them. It is not so among you; whoever wishes to become great among you shall be your servant; and whoever wishes to be first among you shall be slave of all."

Those who would be leader-managers of an organization that serves must begin by being servants themselves. The Greeks have a saying,

> "Oh teacher who hast taught—
> But failed to follow your own teachings!"

It is the behavior of the leader-managers of an organization that determines quality. It is their positive outlook and concern for their customers which generates a service-oriented culture.

AUTHORITARIAN VS. DEMOCRATIC LEADERSHIP

Leadership is the quality that ensures that managers, their associates, and their organization are all moving in the same direction, toward the same destination, at the same speed; not because they have been forced to, but because they want to. This quality is referred to as *influence* in John Maxwell's seminal book *Developing the Leader within You* (Maxwell 1993). Where there is no influence, there is no leadership; and consequently, no participatory management. True leadership is as important an attribute for professionals in service organizations, who must gain the respect and recognition of their customers, as it is for community leaders and small businessmen. Little progress can be expected when Hodja or other *nikokiris* or managers refuse to ride backward on their donkeys when the occasion demands.

The Greek language has two words for "leader": *Ygetis* refers to a natural leader, while *archigos* suggests an appointed leader or one who grasps the position by force. The difference in their meanings became clear when a group of youth club leaders attending a seminar on leadership was asked to name some of the great leaders in history. Their list of names included:

Churchill, Hitler, Pasteur, Madame Curie,

Karamanlis, Alexander the Great, Roosevelt,

Napoleon, Venizelos, MacArthur, Mother Teresa

The seminar members, in reviewing the list, recognized that Churchill, Karamanlis, Venizelos, Pasteur, Madame Curie, Roosevelt, and Mother Teresa gained their positions of leadership by popular acclaim, based on certain innate or acquired qualities. Each was an *ygetis*, a natural leader. The authoritarian leaders—Napoleon, Hitler, Alexander the Great, and MacArthur—either were appointed or took leadership positions by force.

LEADER-MANAGERS

Some managers may become successful natural leaders because of their personal attributes even though they originally gained their position through appointment, inheritance, or force. The more the manager of a service organization applies the principles of democratic or participatory leadership, the more successful the program will be. Professor Arlen Etling has carried this concept one step further (see Chapter 3, pages 30 and 31). He introduces the concept of *facilitator leadership* in which the leader studies a situation, decides what style of leadership is needed, and acts accordingly (Etling 1994).

The use of the word leader as part of a collective noun, leader-manager, clarifies the type of manager most effective in a service organization. A *leader-manager* is one who applies democratic leadership principles while recognizing that there will be occasions that call for facilitator leadership. This definition poses two questions: How can managers of urban or rural service organizations be trained to become leader-managers? How can *nikokiris* leaders in a community be trained to become more competent leader-managers?

TRAITS OF A LEADER-MANAGER

The YMCA and the YWCA have devoted decades to training both professional and volunteer leaders. Jerold Panas, a YMCA and YWCA consultant who has spent many years working with volunteers and professionals in fund raising and campaign management, summarized his observations on leadership, which have been paraphrased here for leader-managers:

"A leader-manager is willing to take the risk, the blame, the brunt of the storm.

He has the power to persuade and inspire others to heights they thought unattainable.

A leader-manager has the heart and the mind to make decisions quickly and decisively. There is a scourging honesty to all he does, a talent to cooperate and coordinate. When he speaks, others listen. He ignites sparks that propel others to action.

When Aeschines spoke, they said: 'How well he speaks. What glorious words.' But when Demosthenes spoke, they shouted: 'Let us march against Philip, now.' Such is the quality of leadership" (Panas 1981).

LEADER-MANAGER CHARACTERISTICS

There is a mistaken assumption that a manager will naturally become a leader by virtue of appointment. This supposition is as erroneous as the converse conclusion that a strong leader will necessarily become an effective manager. One of the most urgent requirements for managers, whether they are newly appointed or have been in positions of management for an extended period, is leadership training.

Appointed managers do not automatically become strong leaders, just as strong leaders do not necessarily become effective managers. They, too, require extensive management training. Most managers are endowed with leadership qualities, but it is important to determine whether they are of an authoritarian, *archigos* style, or democratic, in the *ygetis* mode. Leaders may have a variety of management skills; but here, too, it is important to clarify whether they include all the skills required of leader-managers.

THE SEVEN LANGUAGES OF LEADER-MANAGERS

Describing leadership and its role in urban or rural service organizations is difficult because of its manifold qualities. Two individuals who embodied many of these and had an inestimable impact on the Farm School's growth were Theo Litsas and Avrilia Vlachou. Litsas, who was associate director of the School, played an especially dynamic role in shaping its course. The reader wishing to better understand Litsas may want to re-read the Dedication at the beginning of this book. Avrilia, who later became Sister Gavrilia, a Greek Orthodox nun, helped to found the girls' school at the American Farm School shortly after World War II (Gavrilia and Gangakis 1996). She taught students the "five languages of leadership" which Litsas put into practice throughout his life. The sections that follow illustrate the contribution of inspired leader-managers such as these to a service organization.

SISTER GAVRILIA'S LANGUAGES

Sister Gavrilia spent considerable time in India working with lepers. She had not been able to master the many dialects and languages because her patients came from different parts of the country. After she had been there two years, an Anglican bishop asked her if she had learned the language of the "natives." Embarrassed to admit that she had not, she hesitated for a moment and then said to the bishop, "Oh yes, your Grace. I have learned five languages." He looked surprised as she went on:

> "the languages of smiling,
> weeping,
> touching,
> listening,
> and loving."

We subsequently added the languages of *praying* and *praising* to Sister Gavrilia's original five. Learning Sister Gavrilia's seven languages is essential to becoming an effective leader-manager in a service organization.

THE LANGUAGE OF SMILING

Like all successful leader-managers, Theo Litsas was never without a laugh and a story. He worked all day and half the night. More than anything, he brought fun and sheer delight into the game of life to those who lived and worked with him at the Farm School. It was he who told the tales of Hodja to the staff. Every time a difficult or frustrating moment came, he seemed to have a Hodja story to match the occasion. He recognized that a sense of humor was vital to running an institution. He also knew that it involved much more than laughter and jokes.

Most managers of service organizations are apt to take themselves much too seriously. In their eagerness to accomplish their objectives, they lose their ability to laugh at themselves and the world around them. When new young staff members became frustrated by lack of progress at the Farm School, they were introduced to Harvey Mindess's analysis of a sense of humor. It often helped them understand the mental attitude associated with the language of smiling: "A cluster of qualities characterizes this peculiar frame of mind:

- *flexibility*, in this case an individual's willingness to examine every side of every issue and every side of every side;
- *spontaneity*, the ability to leap from one mood or mode of thought to another;
- *unconventionality*, an individual's freedom from the values of time, place, and profession;
- *shrewdness*, refusal to believe that anyone—least of all oneself—is what he or she seems to be;
- *playfulness*, the grasp of life as a game, a tragi-comic game that nobody wins but that does not have to be won to be enjoyed" (Mindness 1971).

Above all, leader-managers need to cultivate a sense of humor about their work. This may not necessarily come naturally, but reflection on a Hodja story or its equivalent has been helpful to many in facing complex problems. Fran London, editor of the *Journal of Nursing Jocularity*, points out that:

"Nurses and other health care professionals are exposed to some facts of life that most people don't encounter, death and dying, bodily (and social) illness . . . The health benefits of a good laugh are incontrovertible: It lowers blood pressure, relaxes muscles, reduces pain and improves mood and perspective . . . A lack of humor can be a sign that something serious is going on. If you don't treat it, you will continue to suffer from it and it could kill you. Or it could even kill your potential for joy" (London 1995–96).

THE LANGUAGE OF WEEPING

Compassion is an integral quality of being a leader-manager. Its role in a service organization is particularly important among staff and volunteers. Trainees come with their own worries, fears, and sometimes tragedies. If leader-managers do not take time to listen, their associates will not pay attention to what their leaders want to tell them. The late Henri Nouwen, a Dutch Jesuit priest who taught at Yale and Harvard Divinity School, describes the compassion of a spiritual being:

"Across all barriers of land and language, wealth and poverty, knowledge and ignorance, we are still one, created from the same dust, subject to the same laws and destined for the same end . . . His flesh is my flesh, his blood is my blood, his pain is my pain, and his smile is my smile. There is nothing in me that he would find strange, and there is nothing in him that I would not recognize" (Nouwen 1982).

In addition to its programs for Greek young people and adults, the Farm School operates an international summer program for predominately American urban teenagers to work in a Greek village. One summer soon after forty campers had arrived from abroad, word reached the School that the brother of one of the boys had been killed in an automobile accident. A small group met to discuss how to help the bereaved brother but felt inadequate because they did not know him very well. One commented,

"You have to laugh with someone before you can cry with him."

Successful leader-managers of any organization learn to laugh with their associates and their clients so that they can cry with them too.

THE LANGUAGE OF TOUCHING

People seldom realize how powerful the physical aspects of a greeting can be. Westerners in particular seem reserved in their salutations. The Hindus in India welcome a person with their hands in a position of prayer, saying *"Namaste"*—"I worship the God in you"—and seem to greet the whole being. Greek villagers are unsurpassed in their welcome, throwing their arms around the visitor as if he or she were the most important person in the world. The Greeks use the term *angalia*, a word which has been variously translated as hug, embrace, squeeze, press close, love, catch hold of, be near to, cling, fold in the arms, clutch, envelop, enfold, nestle, cuddle, press to the bosom, and snuggle.

Leader-managers reach out to touch and hug with more than their hands. They do it with their eyes, their voice, and most of all with their ears when they listen attentively. Education often seems to inhibit touching and *angalia*. Foreign teenagers who live with Greek families never forget the warm embracing of their Greek mother and father, some of whom may not be able to read or write.

Theo Litsas made a profound impression on people when he greeted them. He put his whole self into his greeting—his eyes, his smile, and his whole face; his outstretched right hand extended toward the other person while his left reached up to the visitor's shoulder. The Farm School has a tradition of sharing handshakes at special gatherings, which gives students, staff, and guests an opportunity to look into each other's eyes and share the warmth of the other person as a greeting or farewell.

THE LANGUAGE OF LISTENING

Listening intently is as important for a leader-manager as speaking—an attribute of which Theo Litsas was fully conscious despite his dynamism. He could lead a dance, a song or a game, but he could also follow and listen—not just briefly but for an hour or an evening—no matter how busy he was. Long after he died, students and friends remembered occasions when Litsas had taken time to become sincerely involved and concerned about a personal problem one of them had discussed with him.

Litsas's ability to listen intently with transparency won him great respect and affection. When leader-managers speak to those they want to help they must open themselves to the language of the brother which not only speaks, but listens and loves. Their ability to use the language of listening, so important for any leader-manager, distinguished Theo Litsas and others like him.

The letter from an individual seeking leadership from a leader-manager can be used to illustrate the meaning of listening. Rather than hearing what a customer or associate is saying, leader-managers often feel compelled to act, to bring about change, to see tangible results. These managers fail to understand how much the individual needs someone who really cares, who demonstrates concern by listening, and who can help others actually solve their problems themselves.

Dear Leader-Manager,

When I ask you to listen to me and you start giving advice, you have not done what I asked.

When I ask you to listen to me and you begin to tell me I shouldn't feel that way, you are trampling on my feelings.

When I ask you to listen to me and you feel you have to do something to solve my problem, you have failed me, strange as it may seem.

Listen! All I asked was that you listen, not talk or do—just hear me.

And I can do for myself. I am not helpless. Maybe discouraged and faltering, but not helpless.

When you do something for me that I can and need to do for myself, you contribute to my fear and inadequacy.

But, when you accept as a simple fact that I do feel what I feel, then I can quit trying to convince you and get about the business of understanding what's behind this feeling, even if it is irrational.

And when that's clear, the answers are obvious and I don't need advice.

Thanks for listening.

Gratefully,

Your friend, who seeks your leadership.

(Adapted from an unpublished statement by Dr. R. A. Hatcher, Georgia State University, Athens)

THE LANGUAGE OF LOVING

Of Sister Gavrilia's five languages, perhaps the most difficult to describe is the language of loving. The leader-manager's love must be akin to J. P. Morgan's comment on the cost of owning a yacht:

"If you have to know how much it costs you, you cannot afford it."

Leader-managers' real challenge is to love themselves out of a job. They have to give totally, expecting nothing in return. Some customers openly convey their appreciation; but leader-managers should not be surprised to sense scorn and contempt from others. The real satisfaction for staff in a service organization should grow out of following the progress of their customers rather than expecting gratitude from them. There is a pillow in the guest house of the Farm School crocheted by a friend, quoting an oft-used phrase by Henry Hope Reed, a longtime trustee, friend, and resident of the Farm School. It reads:

"No Good Deed Goes Unpunished"

Many visitors to the School consider it a rather fanciful comment, but one that is illustrative of how important it is that leader-managers at all levels must learn to laugh at themselves and not be constantly expecting gratitude for what they have done to help others. There is a somewhat similar Chinese saying—"Why do you hate me? I never gave you anything free!"

One of the best descriptions of the language of loving comes from St. Paul's First Letter to the Corinthians, in which I have substituted the word *leader-manager* for the word *love*:

A leader-manager is patient and kind. A leader-manager is not jealous or boastful. She is not arrogant or rude. A leader-manager does not insist on her own way. She is not irritable or resentful. She does not rejoice at wrong but rejoices in the right. A leader-manager is full of trust, full of hope, full of patient endurance. Her work never ends.

THE LANGUAGE OF PRAYING

In her later years, Sister Gavrilia added a sixth language to her original five, the language of praying. Her interpretation tied in closely with Dr. John House's motto (and that of the Benedictine monks):

"To work is to pray."

This spiritual quality gave a special dimension to Litsas's leadership. His Greek Orthodox upbringing, influenced by Quaker thought and Sufi traditions, helped him to understand the integral relationship between work and prayer and to interpret it for the students. The characteristic most common to Theo Litsas and Sister Gavrilia was their capacity to approach the divine in prayer with a fellow human being regardless of religion, culture, or nationality. As with many great leaders, their spirituality transcended dogma in its capacity to reach out and touch the other's heart.

THE LANGUAGE OF PRAISING

When listening to the story of Sister Gavrilia during a seminar in Nepal, one of the participants in the back of the room asked, "Excuse me, I didn't hear you well. Did you say the language of praying or the language of praising?" The response came without much hesitation, "It was the language of praying, but I think we better turn it into seven languages and add 'the language of praising' to the other six." Surely, there is no more important language that can add to the status of leader-managers than their constant use of praise as a means of building the self-esteem of their associates and those whom they seek to help.

CULTIVATING LEADER-MANAGER ATTRIBUTES

There are seven attributes which leader-managers must cultivate just as there are seven languages they must learn to speak. These leader-managers can only learn the practical aspects of leadership by experience. Their leadership roles vary according to the needs and interests of each group with whom they work. They must not only lead their group but also manage programs. A group of Farm School staff once identified seven characteristics that they had observed among leader-managers who aspired to positions of leadership. They then discussed how such leader-managers could be trained.

1. TEACH THEM TO COMPROMISE

Leader-managers may be called upon to supervise other managers, while learning to compromise with associates from other disciplines who are participating in their programs. Depending on the situation, they must be prepared to switch from democratic to authoritarian leadership, sense when to lead and when to follow, and be constantly attuned to the needs of small groups, individual customers, or the larger community. This awareness is every bit as essential for professionals as it is for community leaders.

2. SEEK OUTSTANDING MENTORS

The word *mentor* is derived from the mythical Mentor, Ulysses's most trusted friend, whom the wily traveler left behind to become tutor, sage, and example to his son, Telemachus, in his absence (Homer 1996). Successful leader-managers are those who learn to emulate the best qualities of their role models, adapting their wisdom to deal with current problems. Identifying and helping to train such leaders in a community can sometimes be more rewarding than training associates as professionals. These leaders often have more to share from personal experiences than they themselves can learn.

3. TRAIN LEADER-MANAGERS

Leader-managers inherit a number of leadership traits by birth. They also profit greatly from training, from their parents, and others. There is a false assumption in many cultures that leadership has a charismatic quality that cannot be learned. Quite to the contrary, leadership and management training should be primary goals of service organizations in both urban and rural communities, both for staff, volunteers, and customers.

Under Theo Litsas, the Farm School made an important contribution to rural development through a variety of courses to train leaders in recreation, community organization, and cooperative management. Even priests attending special courses appeared to develop a greater sense of confidence and were eager to try new approaches in order to gain added recognition in their parishes. Building this selfconfidence is a vital element of leadership training.

4. CULTIVATE INNOVATORS

A Farm School staff member working with School graduates in rural communities observed that innovative leaders seldom accept elective positions in the villages. In contrast, those leaders who become community presidents are not generally willing to try untested agricultural innovations. This observation reinforces leadership studies conducted in the United States, which indicate that there are two distinct types of leaders:

1. Innovative leaders are willing to experiment even if they fail. They do not have a large following in the community because they are regarded as eccentric.

2. Group leaders, on the other hand, move ahead of the rest of the community but always at a pace that their neighbors can follow.

Leader-managers should constantly cultivate and encourage innovators around them. Daniel Benor and James Q. Harrison use the phrase "imitable contact farmer" to describe the group leader who makes innovations which other villagers are likely to follow (Benor 1977). They identify another kind of leader when they state, "But these contact farmers should not be the community's most progressive farmers, who are usually regarded as exceptional, so that their neighbors tend not to follow them." Leader-managers in voluntary organizations should follow this same advice. They should seek out and cultivate dynamic innovators among the staff but not necessarily promote them to a level where they have many subordinates until they prove themselves as leader-managers.

5. TRAIN LEADER-MANAGERS AS COMMUNICATORS

Leader-managers must be able to relate to outsiders and speak convincingly. To increase the students' confidence as future leader-managers, the Farm School introduced a public speaking program. Each day, boys and girls are expected to give five-minute talks to the entire student body and faculty. Long after they leave the school, graduates describe their original stage fright, and the confidence they acquired with each successive talk. Invariably, they speak gratefully about the sense of confidence that their public speaking experience at the School gave them. One alumnus wrote, "The daily ten-minute speech by students at the assembly hall early in the morning was really an excellent lesson for me. That was the time when I started facing the crowd without fear, and feeling confident about myself" (Minoudis 1998).

6. RECOGNIZE LEADERSHIP AS BEING SPECIFIC

Leader-managers help others to understand that those who command respect in one sphere are often disappointed when they fail to win support in an unrelated area. It is difficult to help them understand that leadership is associated with expertise in a particular field, with different groups, periods of time, and specific places. It is not usually transferable from one situation to another. Leadership in an organization or community is specific, not general. Wise leader-managers identify their own weaknesses and surround themselves with other leader-managers who can fill the vacuum.

7. CULTIVATE OTHER LEADER-MANAGERS

Leader-managers are faced with a two-fold challenge. They need to broaden themselves to become confident and effective managers. They must also identify and cultivate leader-managers among those with whom they work. Capable leader-managers are continually seeking to improve themselves. They also understand the challenge of inspiring others to become more competent. Leader-managers must recognize that training associates is as important a goal for their own enhancement as it is for those they train. Their ultimate ambition should be to train leader-managers at every level, among professionals, as well as among trustees and customers.

TABLE 6.1 Self-Evaluation Form

CHAPTER 6: BECOME A LEADER-MANAGER Where are you as a leader-manager on the scale: *Kakomiris* (1) . . . to . . . *Nikokiris* (5)?						
TOPIC	1	2	3	4	5	PRIORITY
1. Uses the language of smiling (page 66)						
2. Shows compassion (page 66)						
3. Reaches out to others (page 67)						
4. Is a good listener (page 67)						
5. Demonstrates affection for associates and customers (page 69)						
6. Makes good use of praise (page 69)						
7. Willing to compromise (page 70)						
8. Uses role models effectively (page 70)						
9. Trains other leader-managers (page 70)						
10. Cultivates innovators (page 71)						
11. Trains others as communicators (page 71)						
12. Sees leadership as specific (page 71)						

(Numbers in parentheses refer to pages where subject is mentioned.)

1. For each topic, place an "X" under the 1, 2, 3, 4, or 5 to show where you think you are now as a leader-manager.
2. For each topic, place a "Y" under the 1, 2, 3, 4, or 5 to show where you would like to be.
3. Mark any item where the topic does not apply to your program "NA" (Not Applicable).
4. Under priority, enter a number on a scale from 5 (top priority) to 1 (lowest priority).
5. Identify three or four of your primary concerns on this theme and develop a "POLKA" plan of work to deal with them.
6. List other concerns, share them with your associates, and evaluate them as above.

DECIDE WHO IS IN CONTROL

■ Is it possible to involve the entire staff of an organization in the control process?

■ How can staff in an organization be motivated to participate in its financial operations?

■ How can a voluntary agency assure quality-oriented service to its customers?

"...far better to teach him to love the jug as you do!"

When the son of Hodja's neighbor reached the age of ten, he decided that it was time for the boy to contribute to the work of the household. Each morning he sent the lad to the well for water with the family's prized earthen jug. Just to make sure that the boy would understand the importance of his task, the neighbor would beat him with a bamboo cane that he kept behind the door. When Hodja heard the boy crying each morning and realized what was happening he approached the neighbor. "Why, dear neighbor, do you beat the child when he has done nothing wrong?" "Ah, my good friend, what good would it do to beat him after he has broken the jug?" replied the neighbor. "It would be far better to teach him to love the jug as you do!" responded Hodja with a smile.

CONTROL AS AN ELEMENT OF PLANNING

CONTROL AS A PROCESS

Control is the process of determining the extent to which every part of an organization, small business, or other operation is adhering to an established plan and progressing toward clearly defined objectives. In the eyes of traditional administrators control should be enforced from the top down or by outside evaluators. Like Hodja's neighbor managing his son, these managers feel they must establish a series of procedures which discipline lower-level staff and control their activities. "Far better," as Hodja replied, "to teach them to love the organization!"

Participatory leader-managers emphasize control from the bottom up. This contributes to a sense of responsibility for control by staff at all levels—a sense of belonging on the "team." Whenever one staff member has too much authoritarian control, top management should become concerned.

A management system in which control is based on disciplinary procedures rather than individual motivation is bound to cause resentment among lower-level staff. They react in the same way as Hodja's neighbor's son, resenting unjustified discipline for something they have not done.

THREE ASPECTS OF CONTROL

There are three dimensions to control in management:

1. General control: making sure that the five elements of the POLKA are properly synchronized in terms of overall strategy and smaller departmental and operational POLKAs.

2. Financial control: assuring that all departments are keeping within the tolerances established by the capital and operating budget.

3. Quality control: maintaining satisfied customers by consistently cultivating them and assuring that they are being adequately serviced in terms of the quality of the organization's product and the quality of customer service.

GENERAL CONTROL

Responsibility for control ultimately rests with the top leader-manager, the chief executive officer. The degree to which this control is delegated to all levels within the organization will depend largely on its size, the training of middle- and lower-level management, and the organization's culture—whether it is dedicated to participatory management or not.

TWO-WAY COMMUNICATION

When the number of employees at the Farm School did not exceed sixty, it was relatively easy for the director and his immediate associates to maintain control. Personal relations with the staff were combined with direct supervision by department heads and supervisors. Individual contact provided opportunities for positive encouragement by top management as well as for bottom-up communication. Control was implemented through positive reinforcement expressed by the question, "How do *you* think we are doing?"

This approach is far more effective than one in which the staff members feel that management personnel are continually checking on them. Lower-level staff desire opportunities for communication in both directions. When the number of employees at the American Farm School increased to one hundred, this personal relationship became difficult to maintain. Failure of top management to delegate authority results in loss of interest and consequently less participation of lower staff in the whole process of quality control. As the number of POLKAs in any single organization increases, each POLKA must maintain its own level of control.

Control is even more vital when authority is delegated. Ultimately the responsibility for program evaluation rests with leaders among the customers as well as with the staff of voluntary organizations. The leaders must be able to relate what is being achieved to defined goals. The relationship between customers and staff makes it essential that objectives be stated so clearly that any deviations will be noticed promptly. In this way shortcomings can be identified at an early stage, the necessary adjustments made, and their implementation ensured.

CLEAR OBJECTIVES CONTRIBUTE TO EFFECTIVE CONTROL

Objectives are important in order that staff at every level understand what they are expected to achieve within specified periods:

1. Periodic discussions allow staff members in a variety of positions to review their work.

2. Supervisors and associates above and below as well as laterally are thus able to evaluate overall progress in relation to the objectives.

3. Standards of excellence, which can be measured in terms of quantity and quality, can be agreed upon by the entire staff, including service personnel, laborers, and technicians.

4. The more leader-managers in an organization (or a community) feel that they are contributing, the more successful will be the process of control, and the higher will be the morale of the organization.

5. In an ideal voluntary organization, the manager's personal concern for the staff is particularly important, as everyone is accustomed to being "part of the family."

6. Staff members and volunteers feel threatened by the impersonal nature of structured organizations. This applies particularly to expanding voluntary agencies or small businesses with growing numbers of employees.

7. The problem of anonymity is usually exacerbated by the absence of adequately trained middle management and experienced supervisory personnel.

8. The ultimate purpose of control is prompt corrective behavior. The participation and support of those directly involved produces quicker and better results.

9. The staff can only be expected to participate in this control process if they feel they are an integral part of the management team.

FINANCIAL CONTROL

Volunteers and staff of service organizations must learn how to verify whether their enterprises are generating maximum results at minimum cost while maintaining satisfied customers. The function of management training for staff at all levels is twofold. The first is to help to maintain control within the organization. Like Barba Manoli in the illustration below, they must keep track of stolen apples. At the same time leader-managers must motivate the staff to take the same keen interest in the financial health of the organization as senior managers.

DELEGATE FINANCIAL CONTROL

In any service organization, top management has the ultimate responsibility, but the more responsibility managers can delegate while ensuring adequate control, the more time they will have to concentrate their attention on the staff, program activities, and long-term planning. At the Farm School, the director was originally expected to sign each voucher. This responsibility was subsequently delegated to the associate director, and was later transferred to department heads and the chief accountant.

CREATE TEAM SPIRIT

When authority is transferred from top management to department heads, many staff members question the new system. However, with the passing of time this approach contributes to improved staff morale and involvement for a number of reasons. Delegation ensures that managers and their staff feel both responsible and involved. Because they are closest to the problems, they become more cost conscious and provide practical solutions to these problems since they feel personally responsible for the

Barba Manoli, a peasant in a village near the Farm School, maintained sufficient control of the apples stored in his warehouse to realize that young children were stealing a few each day by spearing them with a sharp pole between the bars. He put up a sign stating that the apples were covered with poisonous pesticides. The next day he found a note from the children who stole his apples. "Don't worry, Barba Manoli. We wash the apples before we eat them."

departmental budget. When such authority is delegated, top management must work with the new managers to help them develop their own guidelines.

1. By following specific procedures and policies, lower-level leader-managers learn to delegate without losing control.

2. Just as they have been empowered by their superiors, they need to identify others in their staff whom they can empower.

3. It is important that in delegating authority they clarify the responsibilities of their associates.

4. New leader-managers need to be aware of the significance of positive reinforcement among staff. They should learn the importance of developing a POLKA for each activity they undertake.

5. They should recognize the value of cultivating horizontal relationships with others at their level within the organization.

6. They must feel confident to turn to superiors for support or counsel when in need of help.

The new system creates a strong sense of team spirit, in contrast to earlier approaches when top management made all decisions. Although delegation would seem to be a relatively simple process, it requires capable and well-organized top leader-managers and department heads prepared to accept and delegate responsibility and authority, and to work as a team. Staff members begin to feel that they are making tremendous progress once this management approach has been initiated. Confidence and intercommunication among employees are essential to this process.

A FARM SCHOOL CASE STUDY

In the sections that follow, some observations on the budgeting process at the Farm School may prove useful. The steps that ensure adequate control through appropriate accounting and delegation of authority deserve consideration. Clearly stated departmental objectives reflect the overall plan of the institution. The budget expresses these objectives in measurable terms. In this way, the budget and its implementation become the definitive tools for control.

The budget is a concrete expression of a POLKA in numerical terms.

Effective participatory planning and review clarifies goals, strategies for accomplishment, and a feeling of group participation rather than control imposed from above. Farm School staff have made the following observations on this approach:

1. Division heads develop a sense of responsibility for administering and controlling their own budgets with the assistance of their staff, who become committed to the final figures which they help to prepare.

2. Day-by-day and week-by-week responsibility for control rests with department heads.

3. Ultimate responsibility rests with the associate director for finance and administration, whose delicate task it is to judge when help or intervention is needed.

4. A series of integrated "K's" from three POLKAs beginning at the department level, and

moving up to the division head, and finally to the organization's overall POLKA, are merged into the final results.

MONTHLY FINANCIAL CONTROL

Financial control comes through the monthly reports issued by the accounting department for consideration by the individual departments. Each report supplies the following information: budget for the year, expenses for the month, expenses to date, and balance. Similar records are kept for income. These reports are turned over to the department head by the tenth of the month for analysis. Responsibility rests with the department head to predict any significant variation.

This technique is referred to as "management by exception": simply put, the associate director is interested only in reports on exceptions or changes from the budget, and not in minor details that the manager himself should consider. The more technicians, lower-level instructors, and other personnel become involved in these discussions, the more they feel that they are an integral part of the whole operation.

QUARTERLY BUDGET CONTROL

Every three months, after consultation with their staff, the managers submit their estimate of the anticipated year-end results based on the results to date. Thus in September, November, February, and May, the budget originally submitted in February is updated and presented to the Board. Revised estimates are based on a review of both the previous fiscal year and the current year to date. The cash flow statement is equally important to predict cash deficits. On more than one occasion, the School has come perilously close to financial collapse because of its failure to anticipate significant demands on the cash flow in excess of what had appeared in the operating budget.

PARTICIPATORY QUALITY CONTROL

The quality of the product of service organizations is *service to its customers* in one form or another. Overall supervision of the quality of this product must ultimately rest with the larger POLKA, which is the sum of its components (the smaller POLKAs throughout the organization.) However, leader-managers should inspire their associates, (staff, volunteers, trustees, and customers) in order to assure participation by all members of the organization in ongoing control of this product.

A PHILOSOPHY OF QUALITY MANAGEMENT

Some of Deming's exhortations to leaders in industry and commerce expressed his well-known Fourteen Points. The Fourteen Points, which outline "a philosophy of management," deserve consideration by aspiring leader-managers eager to introduce the quality approach into their operation. Excellent summaries of Deming's work by Mary Walton (1986), Gabor (1990), and Richard Williams (1994) provide the basis for the following interpretation and arrangement of twelve of these fourteen points as they apply to voluntary agencies.

1. *Eliminate dependence on periodic or terminal inspection by outside "experts."* Quality and service to the clients must not be something that is measured "after the fact." It must be looked upon as an integral part of the ongoing process requiring continual evaluation

by the organization's customers whom it has been established to serve (Chapter 2). Identifying mistakes after the completion of a project does little to help the program's clients.

2. *Emphasize constant improvement in the program of service to the organization's clients.* Everyone in the organization must be convinced that what is good enough for today is not good enough for tomorrow. There must be room for what John W. Gardner refers to as "Self Renewal" in an innovative society (Gardner 1964). Constant improvement means that no standard of achievement should be binding on the future. Levels of quality realized today must be the basis for future improvement. Established, unchanging standards can be the death of an organization.

3. *Institute effective training.* This does not refer to broader academic education alone; the professional and the volunteer should be trained to do his or her job more effectively. Training should relate directly to the job, and include not only staff and volunteers, but also the clients themselves. The variety of competencies included should relate to the goals of both the organization and the members of the community being served. In rural development, this has the same implications as what Chambers refers to as "putting the Farmer First" (Chambers, Pacey and Thrupp 1989).

4. *Eliminate fear.* Fear can be a critical stumbling block for implementation of participatory management at all levels. When professionals, other employees, or clients fear the effects of speaking out, taking risks, or asking questions, the possibility of improving quality or increasing participation in the process is drastically reduced. Managers who rule by fear, either through the administration of punishments or by granting special favors, create a climate of perceived unfairness (Williams 1994, 9). During more than 450 years of Turkish occupation, a favorite expression used by Greeks and Turks alike was, "Does a donkey fly?" "If *you* (the occupying power) say so, of course he can fly!"

5. *Eliminate barriers between departments.* Although competition between departments or cooperating and parallel organizations might appear beneficial, in the long run it can lead to conflict and stifle cooperation. There is a Greek expression:

> *"There is nothing so unchristian as a Christian doing business!"*

It is often used in relation to competing church organizations. A far more appropriate saying is:

> *"Each hand washes the other, and both wash the face together."*

Complex organizational charts (especially those with a multitude of dotted lines) have a way of creating rather than eliminating barriers.

6. *Eliminate slogans and exhortations.* During the years prior to World War II, Greece underwent a series of changes in its system of government. Each new government would come out with new slogans and goals, not very different from those of the previous ones.

> *"Emmanuel changed his clothes," said the cynical citizens. "He put them on inside-out!"*

Dictatorships and authoritarian managers often introduce slogans to motivate people to action. They in fact have little or no impact upon unbelieving populations or employees. Two such slogans, "A place for everything, and everything in its place" and "Everything unto a mean" (from classical Greece) were often repeated at the American Farm School. They eventually acquired a hollow ring. Far more effective was Director Charles House's habit of wearing overalls in the shops that prompted others to follow suit.

7. *Eliminate numerical quotas.* Numerical quotas have a way of interfering with pride of workmanship and quality of relationships. They also encourage superficiality in communication between professionals and clients or among "competing" managers. "How many" replaces "how good" or "how effective" (Williams 1994, 10) as a measure. Numerical goals emphasize increasing quantity at the expense of improving quality. Exceeding the expectations of those we are seeking to help with regard to quality of relationship has far greater long-term value. Increasing the numbers of innovations introduced or individuals contacted does not impress customers unless these increases are accompanied by quality of relationships.

8. *Eliminate barriers to pride of workmanship.* Most people want to do a good job. They do not want to receive unjust criticism or be inaccurately judged. Their minimum expectation is to be treated fairly. Annual performance appraisals that focus on negative generalizations can destroy a desire for improvement. A participatory environment requires leader-managers who encourage workers to do their jobs well and to the best of their ability. This differs considerably from a system that achieves compliance through intimidation (Williams 1994, 10).

9. *Institute a vigorous program of education and improvement.* It is vital that professionals, volunteers, and clients alike are thoroughly familiar with the tools and techniques of participatory management. These tools and techniques applied by leader-managers become the means of communication and improvement. Combined with efforts to develop new methods of teamwork and of sharing, they can lead to the adoption of a new philosophy of participatory management as a part of the organization's culture.

10. *Take action to accomplish the transformation.* A small group of enthusiasts is not enough to implement a plan of participatory quality management in development. Commitment is required from everyone in the organization. Trustees and top management must be committed, but even they cannot succeed without the enthusiastic support of the professionals and volunteers working in the field.

11. *Avoid the use of annual performance evaluations to judge volunteers or staff.* They are bound to be counterproductive. Better to use performance evaluations as a basis for praise and encouragement.

12. *Assure a long-term commitment by both professionals and volunteers.* It is important that leader-managers in many voluntary agencies see themselves in the "midwife role" of working themselves out of a job. By the same token, it is a mistake to change leader-managers every two or three years, just as they learn local customs and develop a close personal relationship with the people whom they are serving. Only then can they really become fully aware of program goals and problems and become better equipped to deal with them positively.

SELF-EVALUATION AS A TOOL OF CONTROL

At the end of several chapters in this book is a self-evaluation form. Its primary function is to help leader-managers, staff, and the organization's customers join together (or work individually) in an exercise of self-evaluation and quality control. No doubt, in reviewing many of the items listed in each questionnaire, those filling it out might make the comment, "What is meant by that phrase?" Most of the items listed grow out of the text. What is meant by the phrase is not as important as what the individual or the group working together on the self-evaluation agree that it means.

If a team were to sit down and prepare such a self-evaluation, they would probably come up with a similar list of items. There is a provision for the team to eliminate any items they feel are not applicable or to add new ones. Obviously all the desirable changes identified by the self-evaluation cannot be implemented at the same time. Where a group is participating, the priorities can be averaged. The next step is to decide how to adjust— the subject of the following chapter.

TABLE 7.1 Self-Evaluation Form

CHAPTER 7: DECIDE WHO IS IN CONTROL Where are you as a leader-manager on the scale: *Kakomiris* (1) . . . to . . . *Nikokiris* (5)?						
TOPIC	1	2	3	4	5	PRIORITY
1. Assures two-way communication (page 77)						
2. Clarifies objectives at all levels (page 78)						
3. Delegates financial control (page 79)						
4. Creates team spirit (page 79)						
5. Encourages participatory quality control (page 81)						
6. Assures evaluation by customers (page 82)						
7. Training for all staff (page 82)						
8. Eliminates fear in evaluations (page 82)						
9. Reduces departmental barriers (page 82)						
10. Avoids numerical quotas (page 83)						
11. Encourages pride of work (page 83)						
12. Avoids judgmental evaluations (page 83)						
13. Assures long-term commitment (page 83)						

(Numbers in parentheses refer to pages where subject is mentioned.)

1. For each topic, place an "X" under the 1, 2, 3, 4, or 5 to show where you think you are now as a leader-manager.
2. For each topic, place a "Y" under the 1, 2, 3, 4, or 5 to show where you would like to be.
3. Mark any item where the topic does not apply to your program "NA" (Not Applicable).
4. Under priority, enter a number on a scale from 5 (top priority) to 1 (lowest priority).
5. Identify three or four of your primary concerns on this theme and develop a "POLKA" plan of work to deal with them.
6. List other concerns, share them with your associates, and evaluate them as above.

8

ADJUST FOR FLEXIBILITY

■ How can leader-managers maintain a dynamic equilibrium within their organizations?

■ Why must leader-managers assure maximum communication at all levels to promote flexibility?

■ How can leader-managers adapt management practices to changing environments?

"Turn it around and adjust it any way you want!"

One day Hodja decided to build a dome-shaped oven behind his house, common to those in the area. When he was two-thirds finished, a neighbor stopped by and pointed out that the opening of the oven facing south would result in burned bread in the summer. Hodja tore the oven down and rebuilt it facing north. Another neighbor stopped by commenting, "Hodja, don't you know the winter winds will blow in and cool it off. It will never bake bread!" Again he dismantled his new oven and built it facing east, and eventually west, with identical results. Finally, Hodja built his oven, covered it with a large sheet and invited his neighbors for the formal opening. When he removed the sheet, to their amazement they saw the oven was mounted on his two-wheel cart. "Now you can turn it around and adjust it any way you want!" cried a somewhat frustrated Hodja.

ADJUSTMENT AS PROCESS

Flexibility, the subject of this chapter, is one of the most important elements that contribute to a leader-manager's ongoing success. Organizations need balance and stability as an integral dimension of their growth. Adjusting is the process by which leader-managers at all levels take corrective action to ensure that original objectives are being met, or modified to meet changing situations. Managers in Greece often quote Hodja's response to his neighbors when they receive clashing advice from trustees, associates, and customers. Hodja's tale may appear extreme, but reference to his solution relieves tension when too many conflicting opinions are expressed.

There are three aspects of management on which leader-managers must concentrate to assure flexibility:

1. Leader-managers should maintain dynamic equilibrium.
2. Leader-managers must maximize communication.
3. Leader-managers should prepare for contingencies.

MAINTAIN DYNAMIC EQUILIBRIUM

SEEK EQUILIBRIUM IN MANAGEMENT

There are three interrelated forces at work in any organization—*policy*, *program*, and *budget*. The Board of Trustees (or other policy-making body) is responsible for appointing the manager and approving policy recommended by the administration. Staff employed by the organization is responsible for implementing the resulting programs. The financial officers prepare and maintain control of the overall budget. It is the responsibility of the top leader-manager, the chief executive officer, to maintain a balance among the three. According to Professor Tad Hungate, Treasurer at Teachers College at Columbia University, if any one of these three centers of authority dominates the other two, some type of adjustment will be required.

THE EQUILATERAL TRIANGLE OF GOVERNANCE

The concept of the equilateral triangle has proven very helpful to Farm School administrators. It is particularly useful to managers of service organizations where communication problems often develop among the Board of Trustees, leader-managers, program staff, and finance directors.

According to this approach, the three centers of power in institutional management should be in a state of dynamic equilibrium as represented by an equilateral triangle (Figure 8.1). The leader-manager of the program, as "conductor," is responsible for coordinating the three groups involved in management so that each understands and respects the other's plans and objectives.

FIGURE 8.1
A Balanced Organization

At various times, one of the three elements may become dominant over the others, causing an imbalance in the organization. When board members attempt to dominate programs, staff activities, and budget details, employees become demoralized and friction grows within the institution (Figure 8.2).

In situations in which the staff becomes dominant, the organization is dominated by the needs of the program as seen by the staff without concern for either policy considerations or budgetary limitations. Trustees become frustrated, lose interest, and fall short in their efforts to raise the funds needed to finance the program. By disregarding the budgetary implications of their actions, the staff brings the organization to the verge of bankruptcy, causing outsiders to lose confidence (Figure 8.3).

When the fiscal officers insist that financial considerations must dominate both policy and program, the staff and trustees become demoralized (Figure 8.4)—none of them feel they play any part in the decision-making process. Financial officers in such positions often take pride in creating large financial reserves, but fail to understand the damage they are causing to morale in the organization.

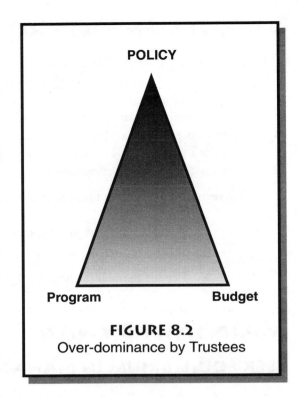

FIGURE 8.2
Over-dominance by Trustees

Leader-managers must continually evaluate the relationship among these three forces and adjust any imbalance in order to ensure a harmonious interdependence. Anyone who has worked with such programs can no doubt cite several that have failed in their mission because the manager had not borne this rule in mind.

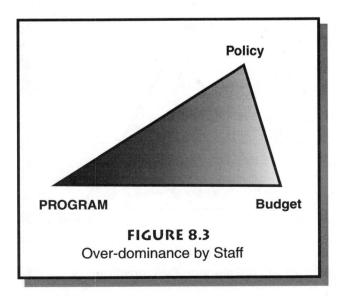

FIGURE 8.3
Over-dominance by Staff

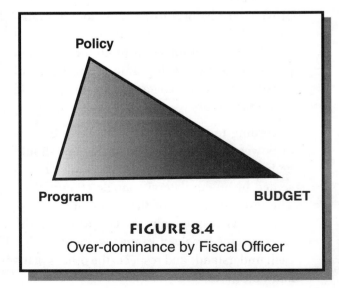

FIGURE 8.4
Over-dominance by Fiscal Officer

ADMINISTRATORS VS. INNOVATORS

Every successful institution or organization needs two kinds of people—administrators and innovators. The administrators organize the operation and ensure that it runs smoothly, while the innovators—the idea people—constantly seek new ways to resolve problems. Without the administrators, the organization soon disintegrates and rapidly heads for bankruptcy. Without the innovators, it will keep repeating the same programs until it no longer serves a purpose. Unfortunately, these two types are directly opposed. The administrators will protect their systems and forms unyieldingly, while the innovators regard them as obstacles to change. To the administrators the innovators seem like dangerous lunatics, while the innovators find the administrators stuffy, unprogressive, and obstructive. The measure of effective leader-managers is their ability to maintain a balance between the two, protecting impulsive, creative innovators from the just wrath of conservative administrators (Rotary International, Rochester, New York, circa 1950).

ADMINISTRATORS AND INNOVATORS

The tension between innovators and administrators can often become an enormous burden for leader-managers. The interrelationships between these two types of personalities and their vital role in any organization are best expressed by the observations above about administrators and innovators.

CREATIVITY VS. INSTITUTIONALIZATION

Leader-managers can seldom sit back feeling satisfied that they have established an organizational pattern that adequately serves a creative program, a community, an area, or an organization. Recognizing that their organization is in constant tension, they must seek to maintain a balance between administrators and innovators. Private institutions are usually more adaptable than public organizations. Small ones are more flexible than large ones that often suffer from institutionalization and self-interest among the staff.

PROGRAM ADAPTABILITY VS. PHYSICAL RIGIDITY

One factor that contributes to rigidity is the inflexible nature of physical facilities. As activities increase and buildings are added, staff attention is diverted from training programs to operation and maintenance of the physical plant. Parker Lansdale, a YMCA secretary who dreamed of inspiring idealistic young men and women through his organizational efforts, eventually resigned from his position as General Secretary because he found he was spending most of his time looking after buildings and budgets rather than serving youth.

Too large a plant has also burdened the Farm School. Dr. John House started the School with one building. Today it has fifty, many of which are difficult to remodel and require constant maintenance. Proximity of offices, connecting corridors, and even the location of water fountains and coffee and tea making facilities affect human relationships. Just as physical conditions lead to inflexibility, so staff using these facilities fall into daily routines that are difficult to modify.

In Tanzania, the Ministry of Agriculture and a foreign aid group designed a short-course center attached to an agricultural school that we visited. The project was expected to help the school reach out into the community and bring the community to the school. The staff decided to hold the first short course even before the facility was completed. It was an overwhelming success, with lectures, demonstrations, field trials, and visits to student projects. At the end, trainees who were accustomed to spending their time out of doors in the villages were asked if they had any suggestions. They replied that they would prefer to sit on the grass rather than inside the classroom. They had felt uncomfortable inside a building and would prefer to sit closer to nature. This demanded an adjustment even before the first building was fully completed.

MAXIMIZE COMMUNICATION

EVALUATION AS COMMUNICATION

Evaluation should be a guide for future action rather than a measure of past performance. Traditional approaches to personnel evaluation in most organizations use the terms "poor," "good," and "excellent." Applied in this way evaluations become tools to judge past performance and determine whether an employee should be promoted or receive a salary increase. In participatory management, evaluation provides an opportunity for various members of the team to help and encourage others through an interview. The problem most leader-managers face, regardless of level, grows out of a hesitation to share unfavorable observations with associates. The thoughts in "Clear the Air" suggest an alternative.

PERSONNEL EVALUATION

The human element is a vital ingredient of the adjustment process. Leader-managers of organizations should design evaluation

CLEAR THE AIR

There's
nothing
more awkward
than a
misunderstanding
left unresolved.
And nothing more
unnecessary.
It leads
to strain,
tension,
invective,
an atmosphere
that can lead
to open hostility.
Why risk losing
a friend,
a colleague,
a customer?
If you have
a misunderstanding
that is a tempest
in a teapot,
don't let it
blow into a
hurricane.
Take the initiative.
Pick up a phone.
Pick up a
pen.
Or pick yourself
up.
March in
right now
and
CLEAR THE AIR.
(*Speerings* 1987)

ACKER EVALUATION

PART A

1. What is the best thing that can come out of this discussion?

2. What is the worst thing that can come out of this discussion?

PART B

1. These are the things that you have been doing which I would like you to continue doing.

2. These are the things that you have been doing which I would like you to stop doing.

3. These are the things that you have not been doing which I would like you to start doing.

programs that fulfill two requirements. They must:

1. Bring about the desired behavior changes without introducing "fear" and condemnation. Insisting that supervisors periodically fill in a form evaluating an employee, even if they have a chance to discuss it, almost invariably leads to conflict or resentment. How can a leader-manager bring about these desired changes in behavior without introducing a sense of being threatened by a fellow employee or associate?

2. Change evaluation from a top-down procedure to a two-way process that can operate both vertically and horizontally. Use a team approach where every member of the team plays a role in the process. Any two participants working together should have an opportunity to evaluate each other—not in a sense of "good" or "bad" ratings, but in terms of "desired changes in behavior patterns" which might lead to improving the quality of the operation.

TEAM EVALUATION

Stanley Acker developed a most effective evaluation technique used by employees working in pairs. It involves five simple statements (Acker Evaluation above) which are dictated by one member of the pair to the other, and then vice-versa in succession. Each participant should write out his or her response to every statement in advance in preparation for the interview. One participant dictates to the other, "Here are the things you have been doing which I would like you to continue doing, etc." The second participant writes these down, seeking clarification for anything that he or she does not understand. The roles are then reversed with the second participant following the same procedure with the first. The two questions at the beginning (Part A of the Acker Evaluation) are included to help both participants understand the limits of any threat they might feel before or during the interview.

BRING IN A REFEREE

Where participants feel that it would be helpful, a third member may be invited to join the discussion as a neutral referee. When participants reach a point of disagreement, the supervisor will have to state that in view of their differing positions, as supervisor, he or she must have the final word. In such a case it behooves the supervisor to suggest that they review their difference again in three months' time. By writing the other's suggestions as they are dictated, each participant avoids a possible misunderstanding of what the other said. It is surprising how many proposed changes are aired in such a discussion about which the other individual never even understood that there was a problem (Clear the Air, page 92).

OVERCOMING THE WEAKNESSES

The Acker approach to evaluation overcomes a number of weaknesses in the evaluation process.

1. It eliminates the dimension of fear in that evaluation does not relate directly to promotion, demotion, or salary changes.

2. It provides an opportunity for two-way communication engendering more of a team spirit.

3. It assures an opportunity during which both participants can "clear the air," expressing concerns which they have felt. This process moves the evaluation from "I like," or "I don't like," to one of seeking mutually acceptable changes in behavior patterns. Assuming that there is adequate communication, it provides an opportunity to further build a team relationship.

4. If the participants are unable to communicate, it recognizes this fundamental difference, leading them to seek help from a third party.

BEWARE OF MEMORANDUMS AS COMMUNICATIONS TOOLS

A serious shortcoming among leader-managers grows out of their assumption that a memorandum to an individual, a department, or a group of customers, either via e-mail or hard copy, will adequately communicate the message needed to be conveyed. Nothing could be further from reality. Memorandums are useful tools to summarize a conversation or a meeting's conclusions, but should seldom be thought of as adequate substitutes for face-to-face meetings, especially ones relating to changes in fundamental planning.

There is a supposition that the use of e-mail will greatly improve communication among various departments or individuals. This assumes that the sender and receiver are synchronized in their thinking. Although a colon and parenthesis combined ":)" are used to convey "a smile on its side," it is a poor substitute for a twinkle in the eyes and the warmth of a face-to-face chuckle.

PLAN FOR CONTINGENCIES

ADAPTIVE MANAGERS

Traditional institutional managers often fail to recognize the dynamic nature of management, perceiving it as a rigid rather than a changing, active process. Maintaining flexibility in an organization is one of the most challenging tasks of leader-managers. It is equally difficult to help staff, volunteers, and community leaders to be constantly alert to the changing needs of those whom they seek to serve, their customers.

ORGANIZATIONAL CONTINGENCY

There are two aspects to the adjustment process:

1. The organization itself must continually adapt to changing circumstances in its environment.
2. Leader-managers should be prepared to adjust to the rapidly changing culture among the individuals served by the organization.

A plan based on a single set of projections is extremely vulnerable to changes in those conditions. Contingency plans are vital in seeking plausible alternatives to original designs—the "what if" situations. Equally important is the process of gaining commitment and support from key individuals directly affected by the changes.

ENCOURAGE MOBILITY AMONG STAFF

Many inexperienced managers make the mistake of assuming that the abilities of individual staff members will remain static, whereas they usually continue to develop. Leader-managers should distinguish between workers' frustration when their abilities are not adequate for their job and workers' apathy when more capable workers are not stimulated by a job that demands far less than they are able to contribute.

With the passage of time, the abilities, interests, and ambitions of young staff members often grow beyond the requirements of their position. The leader-manager then has two options:

1. Develop new programs that will keep challenging the employees.
2. Suggest that the employees involved move to another institution that can better use their broadened interests and ambitions.

At one time, the Farm School staff tended to be insular and resented those who resigned to join other institutions. They eventually recognized that there was not sufficient scope for all the capable young staff members and that some should leave and others be promoted. Once they accepted the idea that a moderate staff turnover was normal and beneficial to an institution, the morale of those who remained at the School improved.

TEACH MANAGERS TO ADAPT

Two obstacles hinder traditional managers from making rational adjustments to fit changing circumstances:

1. Some leader-managers with years of experience have a characteristic inflexibility that grows out of traditional conservatism and distrust of innovation.

2. Inexperienced leader-managers tend to grow rigid when dealing with problems.

The common phrases used by the *kakomiris* manager, "It can't be done," "You know who I am," and "I understand, I understand" (when they do not) are indicative of their inflexibility. One of the challenges of the leader-manager is to help associates understand the importance of flexibility in management so that they can learn to develop contingency plans and adjust more readily to changing circumstances.

LEADER-MANAGERS LEARN FROM MISTAKES

Nikokiris leader-managers learn the significance of flexibility in management from personal experience as well as through training. The capable small businessman is closely attuned to the slightest changes in prices and market conditions and is able to respond accordingly. Leader-managers have to learn this flexibility through practical experience based on the Confucian precept:

"I hear, I forget.
I see, I remember.
I do, I understand."

There is a phrase often quoted in Greece:

"A wise man is one who never makes the same mistake twice."

EMULATE THE ISRAELI MODEL

The Israeli approach to the development of new agricultural industries deserves study by business and service organizations. In the early 1970s, when the Israeli Ministry of Agriculture made the decision to market cut flowers for export on a large scale, a group of agriculturists was sent to the United States and several European countries. The Ministry insisted that these agriculturists should physically work in the foreign countries to acquire the necessary practical experience. While they worked, they studied how the industry was operated.

At home, the responsible officials found that the best way to ensure continual adjustment was through field trials. Simultaneously, the Ministry organized a program in Israel to train scientists who specialized in diseases, marketing, and other phases of cutflower production. This group cultivated experimental plots and greenhouses, which became practical training grounds for agriculturists and farmers who had not been abroad. Through the joint efforts of specialists, agriculturists, and farmers in both the kibbutz and the *moshav* (cooperative villages), the program was reviewed and adjusted, leading to improved techniques. Cut flowers rapidly became an important export crop.

The guidelines of the Israeli Government in introducing the cut-flower industry deserve consideration by organizations seeking to introduce innovation.

1. Train managers in the new field or seek others with experience.

2. Send the new managers beyond the organization to acquire practical experience.

3. Import top-level experienced consultants from outside to help in the planning.

4. Involve leader-managers at all levels (including, in the Israeli projects, farmers, agriculturists, research specialists, and university faculty) in the training and planning process.

BEGIN NEW PROGRAMS SMALL

Helping small businesses and development programs to understand the process of adjustment has been a concern of the Farm School staff for some time. Some of their guidelines for small businesses beginning a new activity, discussed at an annual staff meeting, might be helpful to leaders of similar organizations:

1. New programs should begin in a small way.

2. It is much easier to make adjustments in a pilot project than in commercial operations.

3. Too many projects are started on a grandiose scale, resulting in a rigid organization because there is so much at stake.

4. By the converse token, the smaller experimental concern can be more flexible.

5. The less complicated a program, the greater will be its chances of success.

MODERNIZE WITHIN THE CULTURE

Leader-managers, regardless of whom their organization is serving, should focus on helping customers modernize within their own culture rather than concentrating on approaches foreign to their own experience. J. Wellington Koo, the Chinese ambassador to the United Nations after World War II, expressed this concept clearly when he told a group interested in development work at the University of Rochester in 1948 that:

> "China needs neither Americanization, Westernization nor Christianization, but *modernization*."

Introducing exotic equipment without adapting it to the local cultural situation creates unimaginable problems. The local people often reject it out of hand. Spare parts are not available nor is it easy to find technicians with sufficient expertise for maintenance. Although there is great value in studying the accomplishments of other cultures, foreign technology must be adapted with caution to local situations. Modernization in inner cities and in developing countries should be thought of as an evolutionary process growing out of a series of adjustments to changing circumstances.

Leader-managers working in organizations seeking to help small business leaders should introduce innovations with caution. They must be made to understand that it is vital for production to be integrated with sources of supply, labor potential, and markets. They should be encouraged to keep returning to the basic steps. Leader-managers in Ireland, who were asked to train apprentices in management, discovered that they benefited greatly from analyzing their own methods in order to explain them to the apprentices. They reported that a constant review of their accomplishments and their methods helped them to recognize the importance of the basics in the growth of their own operations.

BEWARE OF OVERCONFIDENCE

As inexperienced managers make progress in their organization and acquire more self-assurance, they tend sometimes to become over confident. They grow lax in their planning and organizing and in their systems of control—which often leads to disaster. Three years after the Farm School began an experimental program in broiler production with its graduates, more than half of them had failed in the business because they had become careless after their early success and failed to prepare for setbacks such as disease, price fluctuations, and marketing difficulties.

The duality of a person's or an organization's fortunes was acknowledged by the ancient Greeks, who cited two inseparable lesser deities of Mount Olympus. The first, Tichi (fortune), gave happiness, whereas the other, Nemesis, brought divine retribution. The ancient Greeks believed that whenever one "friend" was present, the other was not far away. Leader-managers learning to adjust must also learn to adapt to the fruition of both their most optimistic expectations and their greatest fears. The modern day Greek village expression is worth remembering:

"Things never happen as you want them to,
But nor as you fear that they might."

TABLE 8.1 Self-Evaluation Form

CHAPTER 8: ADJUST FOR FLEXIBILITY						
Where are you as a leader-manager on the scale: *Kakomiris* (1) . . . to . . . *Nikokiris* (5)?						
TOPIC	**1**	**2**	**3**	**4**	**5**	**PRIORITY**
1. Maintains dynamic equilibrium among policy, program, budget (page 89)						
2. Balances innovator/ administrator (page 91)						
3. Avoids institutionaliza-tion (page 91)						
4. Buildings do not limit program (page 91)						
5. Maximizes communica-tion among members of the staff (page 92)						
6. Evaluates to change behavior (page 92)						
7. Encourages two-way evaluation (page 93)						
8. Uses team evaluation approach (page 93)						
9. Avoids memos as communication (page 94)						
10. Plans for contingencies (page 95)						
11. Encourages staff mobility (page 95)						
12. Teaches managers to adapt (page 96)						
13. Avoids overconfidence (page 98)						

(Numbers in parentheses refer to pages where subject is mentioned.)

1. For each topic, place an "X" under the 1, 2, 3, 4, or 5 to show where you think you are now as a leader-manager.
2. For each topic, place a "Y" under the 1, 2, 3, 4, or 5 to show where you would like to be.
3. Mark any item where the topic does not apply to your program "NA" (Not Applicable).
4. Under priority, enter a number on a scale from 5 (top priority) to 1 (lowest priority).
5. Identify three or four of your primary concerns on this theme and develop a "POLKA" plan of work to deal with them.
6. List other concerns, share them with your associates, and evaluate them as above.

9

INSPIRED LEADER-MANAGERS

- What do we mean by *Inspired* Leader-Managers?

- What is involved in generating creativity and dreams which lead to vision and focus?

- How does clarity of thought lead to moral autonomy, meditation, and inner peace?

"Then it really doesn't matter which road you take."

One day Hodja was resting at a crossroads on the edge of the village. A stranger stopped to ask for directions. When Hodja asked him which village he was heading for, the stranger looked hesitant and said he was not really sure. "Then it really doesn't matter which road you take," said Hodja, with a trace of a smile on his face.

WHICH ROAD TO TAKE?

THE SPIRIT PERSON ROUTE

Sooner or later, each of us assigned to positions of management reaches the crossroads where Hodja sat over five hundred years ago, that stage in our lives where many of us have to make a choice among three paths. Many are satisfied to think of themselves as capable administrators in their professional lives. Others are eager to express themselves as leader-managers, applying John Maxwell's definition of leadership as "*influence*" (*the ability to get followers*) (Maxwell 1993). If individuals have no followers, there is no way they may think of themselves as leaders. The third group chooses to establish a role for themselves as *inspired leader-managers*.

THE SPHINX'S RIDDLE

According to Greek mythology (*Bullfinch's Mythology* 1979) there was a riddle posed by a Sphinx to every stranger approaching the ancient city of Thebes where Laius was King. Oedipus, the son of King Laius, had been raised abroad from the time he was a baby, knowing nothing of his heritage. While approaching Thebes, he unknowingly slew his own father. At the gates of the city the Sphinx posed its riddle:

"What animal is it that first walks on four feet, then two, and finally on three?"

To the joy of the terrorized citizens of Thebes, Oedipus confronted the Sphinx and solved the mystery. Mortified, the Sphinx committed suicide. As a token of gratitude Oedipus was given his own mother, the Queen, in marriage, compounding the tragedy. Oedipus's reply to the Sphinx was:

1. "It is man who first walks on his hands and feet.
2. In adulthood he walks self assuredly on his own two feet.
3. In his old age he must depend on a cane as a third foot to maintain balance."

ALTERNATIVE PATHS TO MANAGEMENT

It might be useful to distinguish the differences between the alternative paths available to leader-managers.

1. Administrators depend on established procedures along with related rules and regulations that assure their control of the organization. Their leadership within the hierarchy depends on their titular authority. Like man as a child in the Greek riddle, they choose to walk on all fours, often depending on structure and position to maintain balance as leaders in their organization.

2. Leader-managers feel secure on their two feet in their positions of leadership, but see their role as leading the minds and bodies of their followers without much consideration for their spirit. A YMCA Trustee recently described the physical education director in her organization. "She sees herself as a great coach and 'phys. ed. teacher' but sees no role for herself as cultivating any influence on the spirit of the members in the '*mind-body-spirit*' triangle of the YMCA."

3. Inspired leader-managers choose *The Road Not Taken* in Robert Frost's classic poem first published in 1916 (Frost 1971) and so eloquently developed by F. Scott Peck in his book, *The Road Less Traveled* (Peck 1978).

> "Two roads diverged in a wood, and I—
> I took the one less traveled by,
> And that made all the difference (Frost 1971, 105).

THE THIRD ROAD

Inspired leader-managers discover equilibrium among three roads as managers. The least dynamic is that of the administrative manager based on structure and position. Far more challenging is the road of participatory management, often referred to as the key element in "quality management." The third road, that of the *Inspired* and the *Inspiring Leader-Manager,* is the most challenging, the one that "makes all the difference."

The Greek poet C. P. Cavafy had written a poem about another road called *"ITHAKA"* in 1911, five years before Frost had written his. As in Cavafy's mythical poem, inspired leadership is a destination sought which does not have to be actually discovered to be enjoyed. It is the journey for which Ulysses, the inspired leader-manager of Trojan times, is searching.

> "As you set out for Ithaka
> Hope your road is a long one,
> Full of adventure, full of discovery . . .
> Keep Ithaka always in your mind,
> Arriving there is what you're destined for . . .
> And if you find her poor, Ithaka won't have fooled you.
> Wise as you will have become, so full of experience,
> You'll have understood by then what these Ithakas mean" (Cavafy 1975).

> *. . . it was Ithaka who gave you the experience of becoming an inspired leader-manager.*

INSPIRED LEADERS AS SPIRIT PERSONS

INSPIRED LEADERS

There is a dimension to our lives as human beings and as leader-managers, described by the term *inspired*—from the Latin, *in spirare,* to breath in, "to move or guide by divine or supernatural inspiration" (*Merriam-Webster's Collegiate Dictionary* 1994).

How difficult it is for many of us to understand what is meant by this concept of "being inspired!" We must revert to Brother David Steindl-Rast's reference to "the visionary ascent into the cloud that covers the mountain" as well as the descent into the desert "there to realize the vision step by step" (Steindl-Rast 1994). Inspired leaders must split their time between the cloud that covers the mountain and the desert of everyday administration and routine.

Thomas Merton, the Trappist monk and mystic, created a stimulating metaphor about the inspiration of silence in the forest (Nouwen 1972, 121). His thoughts were paraphrased during a seminar surrounded by the 5,000- to 8,500-meter-high peaks in Nepal to describe those unbelievably rich moments experienced by inspired leaders:

At sunset in the Himalayas,
When the tongue is silent, you can sense the silence of the mountains.
When the mind is silent you can hear the voice of God in the mountains.
When the heart is silent, then the whole range of mountains comes alive and ablaze with
the presence of the Almighty.

SPIRIT PERSONS

Before we proceed to discuss the essential distinctions among the three types of leader-managers, it would be useful to discover what we really mean by an *inspired leader-manager*. A key to this discussion is an understanding of what is meant by a *spirit person* in the context of this book.

Professor Marcus Borg of Oregon State University distinguishes between the concept of *holy man* and that of a *spirit person*, the latter being:

> "a person to whom the sacred is an experiential reality . . . They are people who have vivid and frequent subjective experiences of another level or dimension of reality . . . there being more to reality than the tangible world of our ordinary experiences."

> "Religious traditions do not speak of the sacred abstractly; rather they *name* it—as Yahweh, Brahman, Atman, Allah, the Tao, Great Spirit, God."

> What they (spirit persons) all have in common is that "they become funnels or conduits for the power or wisdom of God to enter into this world. Anthropologically speaking, they are delegates of the tribe to another layer of reality, mediators who connect the communities to the Spirit" (Borg 1994, 32–33).

Obviously, Borg is speaking of ultimate spirit persons. However, there exists within all of us as individually inspired leader-managers the opportunity to experience another dimension of spirituality, one in which the sacred can become an experiential reality.

This concept was developed earlier by Mercea Eliade, Chairman of the Department of History of Religions at the University of Chicago, in his book entitled, *The Sacred and the Profane, the Nature of Religion*. Eliade attempts "to show in what ways religious man attempts to remain as long as possible in a sacred universe" (Eliade 1959, 12–13). He contrasts this spiritual experience of life to that of the man without religious feeling, the one who lives, or wishes to live in a desacralized (profane or secular) world. Some managers, and even leader-managers, choose to live in Eliade's "desacralized (secular)" world while others are eager to seek the "sacred," to discover the spirit person within.

Steindl-Rast refers to the sacred as the mystical moments in which "we learn to savor the world rather than manipulate and use it." He refers to the heart as that sacred

> "center of our being at which we are truly 'together': together with ourselves, not split up into intellect, will, emotions, into mind and body: together with all other creatures, for the heart is that realm where I am paradoxically not only most intimately myself, but most intimately united with all" (Steindl-Rast 1994).

Our challenge in seeking to become inspired leader-managers is to discover the sacred within our lives—the realm of our hearts and souls.

THE PROCESS OF CULTIVATING SPIRIT

Inspired leader-managers begin with *dreams*.

Dreams generate *creativity*.

Creativity leads to *vision*.

Vision promotes *focus*.

Focus contributes to *clarity of thought*.

Clarity of thought stimulates *pursuit of alternation*.

Alternation engenders *moral autonomy*.

Moral autonomy motivates *meditation of the heart*.

Meditation generates *inner peace*.

Inner peace cultivates a *royal generosity of spirit*.

IDENTIFY THE MIRACULOUS VALUE OF DREAMS

There is a miraculous nature to dreams. Howard Thurman described how human beings become their dreams.

> "A dream may be held at the focal point of one's mind and heart until it takes over the total process of one's thinking and planning, until at last a man becomes the living embodiment of what he dreams. This is the first miracle: a man becomes his dream; then it is that the line between what he does and is and his dream melts away . . . The second miracle appears when the outline of the dream begins to take objective shape, when it begins to become concrete . . . and the embodiment of the dream in his life" (Thurman 1953, 41–42).

It is when dreams take on objective shape that they inspire creativity, a willingness to break out of our present paradigms (examples from our own lives) and reach out to the unlimited possibilities that lie beyond our own narrow spheres. As the scientist seeks to explore the farthest reaches of the universe and the minutest microorganisms, so creative leader-managers reach out to every undiscovered dimension within themselves and that of their fellow human beings.

"I have a dream!" said Martin Luther King Jr. in Washington, D.C. "I have a dream!" said Mother Teresa in Calcutta, when announcing her plans for organizing the Sisters of Charity. Nelson Mandela's dream for South Africa was "to liberate all our people from the continuing bondage of poverty, deprivation, suffering, gender, and other discriminations" (Meredith 1997, 521). Creative leader-managers all over the world say "I have a dream!" and set about creating a reality out of their dream.

GENERATE CREATIVITY

There are three steps to the creative process:

1. Inspiration
2. Perception
3. Implementation

Leonardo da Vinci could never have painted the Mona Lisa had he not been inspired by his vision of his model La Belle Jaconde's smile. Michaelangelo could not have created the Sistine Chapel without his inspiration of God reaching out to man. Beethoven could never have written his Ninth Symphony without the inspiration of Goethe's *Ode to Joy* and by the melody of the music that he was never able to hear. So Goethe could not have written his *Ode to Joy* had he not in turn been inspired.

When the American Farm School celebrated its Fiftieth Anniversary in 1955, a young Fulbrighter, Charles Brauner, prepared an anniversary booklet with the opening lines:

As a dream it began
in the heart of a man.
Two hands became many
and a School was born.

John Henry House's dream had been turned into a creative process out of which grew his School. A school or any other organization requires more than inspiration that is perceived in the mind of one man. Implementation demands management and leadership skills, but they must be combined with creative energy. They require an aptitude for creative thinking, creative listening, creative doing, and creative laughter through which the dream, now a vision, can be shared. A dream supported by sound management and inspired leadership rapidly turns into a creative vision.

SEEK INSPIRED VISION

We must revert to the definition of inspired—*"to move or guide by divine or supernatural inspiration."* How does a leader-manager "move or guide by divine or supernatural inspiration?" This brings us back to the requirement that she be a spirit person first and foremost. If the leader-manager has not climbed to the tip of the mountain called inspired management, how can she inspire others to follow in her footsteps?

Inspiring visions appeal to the ethereal places in the hearts of inspired leader-managers, and in the hearts of all those associated with the organization that they represent. At this point there grows a firm conviction on the part of these spirit persons that they have a responsibility to inspire others. This in turn inspires other leaders to attain ever-higher levels of visionary leadership. Orchestra conductors inspire musicians who in turn inspire their *maestros* to higher levels. The spirit person within is driven to new heights of spirituality—finally reaching Maslow's "peak experience" (Maslow 1971), shared not only by the conductors and each member of the orchestra, but by the audiences which become an integral part of the performances.

Remove the spirit from conductor, musicians, or audience and the entire performance is rapidly reduced to a well-synchronized mechanical presentation!

CLARIFY YOUR FOCUS

Without focus, a vision soon loses direction and the "ship of state," the inspired organization, finds itself drifting in a multitude of currents at the same time. Like Hodja's passing visitor, the organization is not sure where it wants to go so it does not really make much difference which route it takes.

Focus expressed by a clear "mission statement" or objective must be communicated at all levels within the organization. Particularly when the leadership is dealing in such terms as spirit persons, there must be general agreement about what the focus is. It demands a meeting of the hearts among the leaders, if not the minds. It is equally important to identify the role of each member in sharpening the focus and finding expression for it through him as an individual. This leaves little room for "it isn't my fault" or "he didn't do it right." The spirit must spread to the heart of every leader-manager within the organization.

Through the communication process there comes a sense of sharing and success while at the same time percolating the focus of the vision among the staff at all levels throughout the organization. This in turn challenges every individual to contribute individually to keeping the dream alive.

PROMOTE CLARITY OF THOUGHT

It is not enough for top management to be clear in their thinking about the vision and focus of the organization. Every member of the team at every level must have thought through his or her own role as a spirit person. They must share the responsibility of generating this spirit among the organization's customers. They must do more than turn to their leaders for inspiration. They, themselves, must identify their own role in promoting this spirit within the organization.

In striving to maintain this spirit, the people at the top are every bit as dependent on their associates throughout the organization as middle-level echelons are dependent on those below them. I have often used a helical spring from a derelict Chinese tractor in Albania as a reminder of Steindl-Rast's metaphor describing the relationship between a mother and her child.

> "The mother bends down to her child in his crib and hands him a rattle. The baby recognizes the gift and returns the mother's smile. The mother, overjoyed with the childish gesture of gratitude, lifts up the child with a kiss. There is our spiral of joy" (Steindl-Rast 1994, 87).

Is not the kiss a clearer expression of thought than the toy? Is not the joy it expresses greater than the joy that set our helix in motion from the top and the bottom?

Mothers as leader-managers as well as leader-managers as mothers must take time to savor the smile of the other and return it in kind. This requires time in an overburdened schedule. The search for time and attention can only be cultivated by seeking alternation throughout the helix.

PRACTICE THE PRINCIPLE OF ALTERNATION

In attempting to harness electricity to transmit power over great distances, electrical engineers discovered that direct current causes a loss of energy in the electric lines in contrast to alternating current. So it is with human energy. Oldham emphasizes this concept in his section entitled, "The Principles of Alternation," in which he quotes Hocking and Von Hugel as well as his own thoughts.[1]

> "God and the world must be worked in with one another forever: forever they must be pursued in alternation."

> "As the body can live only by inhalation and exhalation; and as the mind can only flourish by looking out for sensible material and then elaborating and spiritualizing it: so the soul can live to be fully normal in normal circumstances, only by a double process: occupation with the concrete and then abstraction from it, and this alternately, on and on."

> "Our powers become rapidly exhausted in our work. If we occupy ourselves exclusively

with the world, even for the purpose of serving it, we become worldly, superficial, unreal and ineffective. We soon discover the need for alternation."

"We cannot live well unless there is something in our lives which offers us, from time to time, the possibility of absolute detachment and solitude."

"When we have caught the spirit of this kind of detachment, we discover that the outer dimension of ourselves varies with the greatness of the thing we are over against quite as truly as with the greatness of the thing allied to us."

It is through these moments of detachment, the time we set aside from family, friends, co-workers, customers, the still-born silence of the deeper heart, that we begin to discover the self and cultivate a moral autonomy, one of the greatest challenges for inspired leader-managers.

CULTIVATE MORAL AUTONOMY

It is not enough for those who seek to cultivate a moral autonomy (what philosopher Immanuel Kant referred to as the "moral law within") to bring their wills into harmony with a set of external commandments prescribed by their faith. They must be prepared, on every occasion, no matter how new or unexpected, to react on the basis of an internal set of moral codes of their own accord. They must be so *inspired* that their own response is a natural expression of their own ingrained sense of values.

Inspired leader-managers need to identify themselves with their moral autonomy so that their higher will becomes their own, leading to a spontaneous reaction to any circumstance. In this frame of mind, no deliberate self-discipline is necessary, for the new nature expresses itself in their lives without their knowing. The ultimate purpose of all faiths is not to enforce a set of rules that must be followed with effort, but to impart a spirit that can take the place of external regulations.

Personal growth takes many forms among leaders. There is an underlying direction in this growth among inspired leader-managers. They have learned to measure their benefits, not by the conduct of others, but by the selfless goodness that wells up in their own hearts. For most spirit persons, this is often defined as moral law. Willcocks, in her book, *Between the Old World and the New*, states that:

"The essence of the moral law, in the view of Tolstoi, the essence that makes it God's law, is simple enough: it is just 'give more than you get'—always. But Western morality says that the only principle by which human nature can be got to move is 'get, whenever possible, more than you give.' Tolstoi's achievement is to have brought all the teaching of the Eastern prophets and saints into one formula, the most revolutionary that was ever devised."[2]

If every inspired leader-manager of every voluntary organization could be motivated to live by Tolstoi's principle, *give more than you get—always,* then surely this would be a far richer world in which all of us could live.

Gordon Smith, the former Chairman of the Monterey Maritime Museum, expressed this concept most graphically to me in Monterey, California, in March of 1992:

"My most prized possessions are those I have given away."

Slowly we learn to share what we have, alternate between a having mode and a being mode, where what we are is more important than what we have. It is then that we discover within ourselves what

Dag Hammarskjold (1964) once referred to as the place within us, the "center of stillness surrounded by silence."

PRACTICE MEDITATION OF THE HEART

How can you "give more than you get"? This question was asked of me on three continents. The three questions in the box below can be summarized in another phrase: "How can we become inspired leader-managers at all levels within our organization?"

HOW CAN WE BECOME INSPIRED LEADER-MANAGERS?

1. In Malawi in Africa: "How can you inspire government organizations who may know the theory of development to apply it in practice as effectively as voluntary agencies who may not know the theory, but far outshine government organizations in practice?" (Interview with Dr. Stanley Kaila, Director of the Social Science Research Institute, Zomba, Malawi, 1993)

2. From Sweet, Idaho, U.S.A.: "How do individuals or voluntary agencies avoid becoming jaded (worn and tired)? How do you keep the sap running in the tree?" (Discussion with Professor Vickie Sigman, Consultant to FAO, Lilongwe, Malawi, 1993)

3. From Korça, Albania: "How do we touch the hearts of our students? How do we inspire them to take pride in their work, to believe in themselves and the future of their country?" (Comment by Pavli Mykerezi, Director of the Korça Agricultural School, Albania, 1997)

Individuals in four inspired voluntary organizations on four continents gave me partial answers, shown in the box on the next page.

Inspired leader-managers of all faiths within all organizations can discover a meeting of the hearts through joint meditation, seeking to discover the "God within." They can search within themselves and among associates bringing inspiration to all the staff and customers alike. We are constantly reminded of the greeting we heard so often in Nepal. Total strangers used it: "*NAMASTE!*"—"I worship the God within you." This state can best be described as *inner peace*.

SEEK INNER PEACE

What do we mean by inner peace? Most people equate this concept with *peace of mind*, having friends, being with family, sensing success about work, and feeling healthy. As important as these qualities are, they only reflect an absence of worry or concern. Inner peace is a far more positive condition, reflecting a sense of oneness with the spirit person within. It is this sense of peace that saturates every cell, the deepest recesses of the body.

FOUR APPROACHES TO BECOMING INSPIRED LEADER-MANAGERS

1. In Nepal, the top management staff of an expatriate voluntary agency, Save the Children/USA, included a Jew, a Hindu, a Buddhist, and a Christian. It was very clear that each of them, regardless of their religious affiliation were *spirit persons* who respected each other's religious beliefs. We did not discuss their spiritual values. They were obvious.

2. In Malawi we met an Anglican, a Methodist, and a Moslem who were vital leaders in the Christian Service Committee. Under their leadership, the Christians and Moslems were working together to help the subsistence level villagers find solutions to their problems.

3. In Honduras we met with the forty leaders of the international development organization, World Vision, to discuss the contents of this book and its application to their program. Each morning, regardless of their religious affiliation, they began the meetings, as they did all meetings, with a period of meditation.

4. More than forty years ago, we had lunch with Athenagoras, the Ecumenical Patriarch of the Greek Orthodox Church in Istanbul. At the time he and Pope John were trying to establish a dialogue between the Roman Catholic and Orthodox Churches. He provided an answer to the question raised by our friends in Malawi, Idaho, and Albania. "When I was in the United States as Archbishop," said the Patriarch, "I learned the meaning of federation. It does not require a meeting of the minds of all forty-eight states—only a meeting of their hearts."

During our seminars in different countries participants are encouraged to select a sponge with a plate of water. They discover that inner peace is like the sponge. As it absorbs the water, every cell is filled. They sense an inner serenity emanating from the peace within, as it spreads throughout every last molecule of the body.

In the fall of 1990 we had a delightful half-hour visit with Mother Teresa in the early evening on her balcony outside her office overlooking the bustling courtyard of her Sisters of Charity Center in Calcutta. We asked her for her insights into what made for an *inspired leader-manager.* She immediately replied, "Teach them to look into each others' eyes with LOVE." As we were leaving at dusk, she pattered in her bare feet into her office, and reached for two cards in her desk which she handed to us. The first one read:

> "Make us worthy, O Lord, to serve our fellow man throughout the world who live and die in poverty and hunger. Give them through our hands the means to earn their daily bread and by our understanding love, peace and joy."

The second note, quoted on the following page, she had signed, "God bless you." On this, our most prized possession, is her philosophy of living as an *Inspired Leader-Manager*.

> The Fruit of Silence is Prayer
>
> The Fruit of Prayer is Faith
>
> The Fruit of Faith is Love
>
> The Fruit of Love is Service
>
> The Fruit of Service is Peace
>
> —*Mother Teresa*

The "fruit" which leader-managers at all levels in voluntary organizations seek is *inner peace,* "the peace which passeth all understanding." A friend asked for a description of Mother Teresa as a model which others might emulate. A few qualities stood out.

A warm and loving smile on her deeply wrinkled face brought a twinkle in her eyes. She felt an inner compulsion to reach out and hold our hands as we sat next to her on the wooden bench. She was alert as a genuinely concerned listener. As an inspired human herself, she was one who exuded a wealth of inner peace, expressed by her genuine affection for people. Her whole Being was a living reflection of a deeply rooted royal generosity of spirit, a vibrant image of her faith in the God within her. She was an exemplary *inspired leader-manager*! She was much more; she was *an inspiring leader-manager.* And that made all the difference to her Sisters of Charity and to the world.

There is an Arabic saying heard in Egypt that surely applies to Mother Teresa. It might serve as a challenge to all inspiring leader-managers who have attained moral autonomy.

> When you were born, you cried,
>
> and those around you smiled.
>
> So live your life, that when you die,
>
> you may smile while those around you cry.

TABLE 9.1   Self-Evaluation Form

CHAPTER 9: INSPIRED LEADER-MANAGERS						
Where are you as a leader-manager on the scale: *Kakomiris* (1) . . . to . . . *Nikokiris* (5)?						
TOPIC	**1**	**2**	**3**	**4**	**5**	**PRIORITY**
1. Seeks spirit person route (page 103)						
2. Chooses the third road (page 104)						
3. Is an inspired leader (page 104)						
4. Cultivates spirit person qualities (page 105)						
5. Begins with dreams (page 106)						
6. Generates creativity (page 106)						
7. Seeks inspired vision (page 107)						
8. Clarifies focus (page 107)						
9. Promotes clarity of thought (page 108)						
10. Practices principle of alternation (page 108)						
11. Cultivates moral autonomy (page 109)						
12. Practices meditation (page 110)						
13. Seeks inner peace (page 110)						

(Numbers in parentheses refer to pages where subject is mentioned.)

1. For each topic, place an "X" under the 1, 2, 3, 4, or 5 to show where you think you are now as a leader-manager.
2. For each topic, place a "Y" under the 1, 2, 3, 4, or 5 to show where you would like to be.
3. Mark any item where the topic does not apply to your program "NA" (Not Applicable).
4. Under priority, enter a number on a scale from 5 (top priority) to 1 (lowest priority).
5. Identify three or four of your primary concerns on this theme and develop a "POLKA" plan of work to deal with them.
6. List other concerns, share them with your associates, and evaluate them as above.

NOTES

1. J. H. Oldham places special emphasis on the need for alternation under a section called "The Principles of Alternation" (First Month, Day 6). In this section he quotes William E. Hocking, *The Meaning of God in Human Experience: A Philosophic Study of Religion* (New Haven, Conn.: Yale University Press, 1944) and Friedrick von Hugel, *Selected Letters, 1886–1924*, First Edition (London: E. P. Dutton and Co., 1927).

2. Oldham had a firm belief in what he refers to as moral autonomy—that individuals should be guided by a spirit which is in harmony with a higher power in which they believe. He quotes Ernest F. Scott, *Ethical Teaching of Jesus* (Macmillan, 1924) and Mary P. Willcocks, *Between the Old World and the New* (G. Allen and Unwin, Ltd., 1925).

BECOME AN INSPIRING LEADER-MANAGER

10

- How can we develop ourselves from Inspired Leader-Managers to Inspiring Leader-Managers?

- What are the stumbling blocks to becoming an Inspiring Leader-Manager?

- What are some of the fundamental skills Leader-Managers need to inspire others?

"One of you will be the Messiah."

As the religious leader of the Moslem Community, Hodja maintained a friendly relationship with the monks of a popular Greek Orthodox monastery nearby. It was a site for pilgrimages by many Christians. As the monks grew older, more quarrelsome and less hospitable, fewer visitors came. The surviving monks wondered what had gone wrong. They decided to invite Hodja to seek his advice. After much discussion with the holy men, Hodja said, "I have learned from my prayers that one of you will be the Messiah." Each of the monks asked himself daily which among the brothers would be the "blessed one." They grew more respectful of each other and of visitors. The pilgrims told friends of the new spirit, praising the holy fathers. Young monks joined the order, repairing dilapidated buildings as a new aura of spirituality spread. Hodja didn't live long enough to discover which monk would become the Messiah. It didn't really matter as he sensed that the spirit had taken root in all of their hearts.

FROM INSPIRED TO INSPIRING LEADER-MANAGERS

THE MAGICAL WAY OF INSPIRING LEADERS

Inspiring leader-managers are often referred to as a "shot in the arm" to floundering organizations searching for their identity. Like the Hodja, such individuals have a magical way of helping the staff to seek their own spiritual identity as well as to become aware of this spirituality among their associates. In some cases these inspiring leader-managers may be invited to participate in short-term seminars. In others, they are hired as permanent staff members within the organization where they are often looked upon as a "breath of spring." There are always small groups of skeptical staff or customers who look upon such individuals with a sense of distrust. Among those who share their optimistic, positive attitudes, they are looked upon as a vital force in the organization.

THE ROLE OF SYNERGISM

There is a descriptive term, *synergism,* derived from the Ancient Greek *synergos* (accomplice) (Pickering 1848, 1252) implying joint energy on the part of all those involved in a task. In Chapter 9 reference is made to David Steindl-Rast's use of the metaphor of the helix to describe the relationship of the mother and child as they reinforce their mutual affection. So all members of an organization who share common aspirations learn to reinforce each other's vision, focus, and dreams.

In the same way inspiring leader-managers as individuals have dreams, so organizations, of which they are a part, have collective dreams. As long as they have dreams in their hearts as individuals or organizations, they cannot lose the significance of living—of their existence. Through synergistic thinking, leader-managers encourage growth on the part of associates who share common dreams. By learning to work together, to meditate together, to reflect together, and solve problems together, they seek some form of higher inspiration. As they do so, they grow individually and as a group, each contributing to the development of the other's character.

THE VALUE OF COMMON DREAMS

At the time of my retirement as the third Director of the American Farm School, in my report to the Board of Trustees I sought to emphasize the importance of organizational dreams. I adapted thoughts expressed by Howard Thurman, once Chaplain of Howard University, Washington, D.C. Thurman described the significance of shared dreams to inspired leader-managers within an organization:

> "The dream is the quiet persistence in the heart that enables the organization, and all those associated with it, to ride out the storms of its churning experiences. It is the exciting whisper moving through the organizational charts and procedures, answering the monotony of limitless days of dull routine. It is the ever-recurring melody in the midst of the broken harmony and harsh discords of human conflict. It is the touch of significance highlighting ordinary experiences, common events" (Thurman 1953).

STUMBLING BLOCKS FOR INSPIRING LEADER-MANAGERS

CHANGING ATTITUDES OF BOARD AND MANAGEMENT

There are a number of factors that lead to a changing attitude among Trustees and management staff. Leader-managers seeking to inspire associates should be aware of these challenges to their efforts. Key factors that bring about this change in the organizational environment are a product of:

1. A growing disinterest among the Board: a failure on the part of Board leadership and top management to cultivate members' involvement.

2. The appointment of new top managers who have a limited interest in the sacred and spiritual qualities which have played a vital role in the organization's early development.

3. Failure on the part of the secular elements among the Board and management to grasp the early flames which first inspired the founders.

4. A tendency among leaders of the Board and top management to look at early values of the organization as anachronistic, "belonging to another time."

5. An attitude among intellectuals on the Board and some management staff to ridicule reference to the spiritual as removed from current reality and "unscientific in the modern age." This is not a short-term process. At Wheaton College in Illinois, it took more than a century for this change in the "saga" (common belief system) to take place (Lansdale 1990).

DISCUSSIONS OF THE SACRED ARE AVOIDED

In most secular organizations talk about the quality of spirit—its sacred elements—is very often avoided at all costs. In his inspiring book, *Care of the Soul*, Thomas Moore builds on his background as a psychoanalyst, describing "psychology as a secular science" in contrast to "care of the soul as a sacred art" (Moore 1994). He quotes the fifteenth-century philosopher, Marsilio Facino, as bringing

"together mind and body, ideas and life, spirituality and the world" (Facino 1980).

People seeking to improve themselves need inspiration as an adhesive—holding together mind and body (and quality of spirit) linking ideas and life, spirituality and their world.

SOPHISTICATED INTELLECTUALS KNOW BETTER

The management staff at the American Farm School was often hesitant to use terms such as "the spirit of the School," "sacred values of the organization," and "the spiritual impact of founder John Henry House." It was particularly awkward to refer to these concepts during formal meetings of the Board of Trustees in New York City surrounded by a number of sophisticated intellectuals who "knew better." In contrast, in Greece, in whatever direction people search at the School, they are continuously reminded of the powerful impact of these qualities on the organization.

THE DREAMS OF INSPIRING LEADER-MANAGERS

Inspiring leader-managers should:

Keep alive the dreams of their ancestors, but remember the flames, and not the ashes.

The dream is no outward thing. It does not take its rise from the environment in which inspired leader-managers move or function. It lives in the inner being, deep within, where the issues of life and death, service to the community, the *re-creation* of the hearts of people are ultimately determined. As long as inspiring leader-managers keep the dream in their heart, they cannot lose the significance of their organizations' existence.

TOWARD BECOMING INSPIRING LEADER-MANAGERS

ACQUIRED SKILLS

There is no end of useful skills deserving consideration by aspiring inspiring leader-managers. It is not enough to understand what these skills are and how they can be implemented. Leader-managers must clarify in their own minds *why* each of these skills is important and how they can be applied to train other inspired leader-managers at all levels among Board, staff, and customers alike.

How can these skills be acquired? It is not unlike tennis players (or other athletes) who are eager to improve their serve. They must spend hours tossing the ball into the air until it is always at the same height. They must be sure that the grip on the racket is just right with the perfect angle relative to the hand. They must practice their swing of the racket—like throwing a ball—until it becomes a natural feeling for them. Only then will they begin to learn to serve. As in all sports, each coach has his or her own theory of what the most important skills are and how they should be taught.

The skills selected are stated in an active verb form, for it is in the doing that the leader-manager will best inspire others to follow. The Greek philosopher, Aristotle, wrote:

"The things which we are to do, when we have learnt them, we learn by doing."
(We are not what we appear to be, but rather that which we repeatedly do.)

Becoming an inspiring leader-manager is not an accident, it is a cultivated skill.

TWELVE QUALITIES FOR INSPIRING LEADER-MANAGERS

What are the key qualities that inspiring leader-managers should aspire to—regardless of whether they are board members of an organization, management staff, teachers, technicians, or even unskilled workers? Regardless of their position, they can become deeply committed to playing the role of an inspiring leader-manager in that position. Many of the suggestions and examples that follow are based on such inspiring leader-managers within the American Farm School over the years. Without living examples, such ideas have little meaning.

1. RADIATE INNER PEACE

Inspiring leader-managers have usually lived through their own *peak experience,* that soul-shaking personal spiritual upheaval which has brought them in touch with the sacred, before they can radiate inner peace. Each in their own way have experienced that moment, or more probably, those moments, out of which they have been transfigured to some degree into spirit persons.

All those who knew John Henry and Adeline Beers House, the founders of the American Farm School, thought of them as inspiring human beings who radiated an inner light in their smiles, their eyes, their mannerisms, and their ability to relate and to listen to others. They reflected a beauty of spirit that inspired their fellow workers. Their sense of wonder appeared to fill them and others whose lives they touched with awe and reverence for life. Their positive outlook expressed a deep sense of appreciation for the gift of their being, and its divine origins. They were guided by, and found comfort in, their spirit within. Peace of mind seemed to lighten their step and helped them stand taller. These qualities touched the hearts of others, helping them in turn to discover their own inner peace and "share it further." These thoughts about the house family were adapted from an inspiring passage in the *Daily Word* (August 10, 1988).

The Vietnamese Buddhist monk, Thich Nhat Hanh, speaks of *Being Peace,* a concept that might be adapted by inspiring leader-managers of voluntary organizations:

> "If we are peaceful, if we are happy,
> We can blossom like a flower,
> And everyone in our family,
> Will benefit from our peace" (Hanh 1987)
> [as will our entire organization].

Robert J. Rawson, a twenty-year-old visitor to the American Farm School in 1920, described this sense of *inner peace* among staff in a letter to his parents.

> "As I came into town yesterday morning I realized that I never before had been in such a literally heavenly place. I'm not using slang. The place, the people, and the work they are doing combine to make one feel good all over and through and through. You can't tell just what does it, but the spirit of the institution grows upon you and fills you with a great peace. Either the place is perfect or I am temporarily blinded."[1]

Very often the blind can see what is essential better than those dazzled by light. How difficult it is for inspiring leader-managers to cultivate this quality of inner peace so that it radiates among associates. Yet how vital this sense of peace is to generating the "spirit of the institution" of which Robert Rawson wrote.

2. COMMUNICATE AS A LISTENER

Leader-managers can use three languages with which to communicate with associates:

1. the *language of the prosecutor* which condemns,
2. the *language of the parent or guardian* which criticizes, and
3. the *language of the brother* which listens.

- Leader-managers soon discover that in communicating with associates of the same educational level, the same cultural and social background, they can use any one of the three.

- Inspiring leader-managers, communicating with individuals of a different educational, social, or cultural background in their organization, limit themselves to the third language: the brother's, which not only speaks, but listens and loves.

What you DO speaks so loudly, I cannot hear what you SAY!

Communicating through listening might best be summarized by three approaches to speaking: SPEAK TO, SPEAK FOR, and SPEAK WITH.

- SPEAK TO: the authoritarian approach of an autocratic manager.

- SPEAK FOR: the language of the parent that never accepts the "child" as grown up.

- SPEAK WITH: the language of the inspiring leader-manager which expresses itself with a listening heart, that "center of our being where we are most fully one with all we are and all that is" (Steindl-Rast 1994).

3. REFLECT SINCERITY

Sincerity is a reflection of those unique qualities that express an individual's identity. Most countries issue an identity card to their citizens, which lists their name, address, occupation, nationality, race, religious affiliation, date, and place of birth, along with their picture. Sincerity is an expression of leaders' identity, as concerns their sense of what is right and what is wrong. They may consciously or unconsciously share this quality with others. It need not be entered on an identity card because it is reflected by the values radiated by the individuals themselves. Such individuals reflect sincerity among their associates, not because of some external constriction, but as a spontaneous expression of a deep-seated motivation.

According to Oldham,[2] Thomas Carlyle defined the challenge facing inspiring leader-managers in 1840:

"Sincerity, a deep, great genuine sincerity,
is the first characteristic of all men in any way heroic."

Oldham quotes William James on this theme: "'Naked came I into the world'—whoever first said that, possessed this mystery. My own bare entity must fight the battle—shams cannot save me."

A deep, great, genuine sincerity is one of the vital characteristics which inspiring leader-managers need to share with their associates.

4. CHALLENGE SPIRITS TO SOAR

The director of one of the most successful YMCA camps in the United States, Bill Briggs, spoke of the need for a staff who behaved "like wild horses—always needing to be reigned in." He sought to inspire this quality among leaders who challenged campers physically, emotionally, and spiritually. "There's nothing worse than staff members who are like horses in need of being whipped into motion," he would say.

The Greek writer Kazantzakis speaks of the challenge in climbing our spiritual mountain. He describes the slow but steady upward pace as we approach the elusive summit. "The highest point a man can attain is not Knowledge, or Virtue, or Goodness, or Victory, but something even greater, more heroic and more despairing: *Sacred Awe!*" (Kazantzakis 1946). Attaining sacred awe should be a primary goal among inspiring leader-managers.

Each summer fifty senior high school students from the United States and other countries spend six weeks at the American Farm School and in a village working on construction projects. Their final goal is to climb to the 3,000-meter peak of Mount Olympus. At the beginning of the summer each participant has as a personal goal to reach the peak. By the end of the summer the goal is no longer, "Will I make it?" but "Will *we*, all fifty of us, make it?" The unity is not limited to reaching the peak, but feeling a deep sense of social and spiritual togetherness as a group. Lynn Claytor, the mother of one participant, wrote to me and my wife:

> "You must know how influential his stay at the School was. It freed his spirit and taught him how rich it is to connect with other people. He grew beyond all previous preconceptions and his spirit now soars with the eagles. He is no longer earth bound."

Nietzsche expressed the challenge in another way: "The most spiritual men, provided that they are at the same time the bravest, experience by far the most painful tragedies; but this is the very reason why they reverence life, because it offers them its greatest oppositions. It is the greatness of the danger that reveals the knight, or rather that creates him."[3]

5. INSPIRE SELF-CONFIDENCE

Self-confidence is like a virus that multiplies and spreads undetected from individual to individual, and then from group to group. It begins, however, with an individual who consciously or unconsciously instills self-confidence among associates.

In 1987 a graduate of the Farm School, George Foundas, wrote to Nico Papaconstantinou, Director of Student Services, a few years after he graduated:

> "I will never forget the best years of my life, those I spent at the Farm School . . . I think that the spirit of the School encouraged one to find the real person inside. The serenity that prevails there, the stillness and beauty of the setting, instill a certain tranquillity within one. It allows you to think about who you really are, where you are headed, what your goal in life is, what are the real values you hold. It is a pity for whoever lives in a place like the Farm School to miss the chance to discover himself, the purpose in life, not to have discovered a way to communicate with God, to find happiness."

Nico Papaconstantinou was not the only staff member at the School who inspired self-confidence in George Foundas. It was also his teachers, the cleaning lady in the dormitory, the cook, his instructors in the practical departments, the receptionist, the night guard, and his dormitory supervisors. Theirs was a synergistic effort that prompted Foundas to finish his letter:

> "Time and distance do not kill love if it is real. To be loved by others is the other half of your loving them. Thanks to all those who helped me."

6. COMMIT SELF TO OTHERS

Inspired leader-managers demonstrate a commitment to their associates by their complete dedication to those with whom they work. This determination to live a life of service grows out of the spirit person within, which plays such a dominant role in their lives.

As Peter Drucker points out, the great spirit persons in history have chosen a small ring of leaders or apostles who have played a key role in transmitting this sense of commitment through their actions throughout the organization. Even among lower echelon staff there are inspired leader-managers who are every bit as committed as those at the top (Drucker 1990, 167).

This sense of commitment was identified by a seasoned Greek government bureaucrat during a one-week inspection tour at the American Farm School. On his final day he addressed the students:

> "I leave now with something inside me, something much greater than I thought was there. What makes this school so special is its sense of commitment, the strong bond that ties the students, staff, teachers, administrators, and their families. I have never been able to experience the feeling of completeness that I felt here—the love expressed through cooperation, common effort, healthy competition, and a feeling of team spirit. The educational climate . . . trains mature human beings with a deep-rooted self-confidence and a faith in their spiritual tradition. The school's personality will be a shining star that will reflect throughout your life."[4]

7. ENTHUSE ASSOCIATES

The term enthusiasm comes from the Ancient Greek, *enthusiazo*, "to be inspired by the divinity" (Pickering 1848, 434). Inspiring leader-managers have a way of "energizing" their associates about life.

In a letter to me, Rob McNeill, now Professor of History at Georgetown University, spoke of the "boost" he and his family received at the Farm School. It was not one inspired leader-manager to which he refers, but the "people . . . manifested at every turn."

> "The Farm School has been a wonderful boost for us. The people who live and work there have been unfailingly helpful, kind, and cheerful. The whole School has a palpable spirit, manifested at every turn, which is in my experience genuinely unique. This spirit of community, cooperation, friendship, enterprise, enthusiasm is normally hard to create, especially in an international cross-cultural setting. Thanks for a chance to see the School's community spirit. If only you could bottle it!"

8. GENERATE A JOYFUL SPIRIT

Oldham felt strongly that humans are created to discover the joy in life even in times of sorrow. Robert Louis Stevenson described the need for a touch of the poet among inspiring leader-managers.

> "The true realism always and everywhere, is that of the poets: to find out where the joy resides, and give it a voice far beyond singing. For to miss the joy is to miss all. In the joy of the actors lies the sense of any action."[5]

Joy is a quality that can be cultivated, even among the most dour leader-managers. It grows out of a deep-seated faith within the human heart. It is a product of a constant effort to seek out the very best within oneself, the spirit person that resides within a man's soul. Where inspiring leader-managers feel they lack this attribute in their own character, they should make an effort to surround themselves with other inspiring leader-managers who do. The primary function of court jesters in medieval times was not just to amuse their sovereigns, it was to bring a lightness of touch, a sense of joy and humor to a potentially dull court life.

St. Francis of Assisi was one of the most joy-filled inspiring leader-managers in history. He made it his dominant goal in life to continually express spiritual joy, both inwardly and outwardly. Equally important to him was to inspire this joy in his brothers. From *The Mirror of Perfection*, Oldham quotes him as saying:

> "Since this spiritual joy comes of cleanliness of heart and the purity of continual prayer, ye should seek above all to acquire and conserve these two things, that ye may possess within and without, that joy" (Oldham 1959).

A young Dutch trainee, Teyle de Bordes, who attended a seminar at the American Farm School, wrote the Director (January 18, 1988):

> "I am writing to thank you for the wonderful time I had at the School. It was very special because of the prevalent feeling of warmth, joy and sharing, the attitude of the students and staff. While at the American Farm School I underwent a 'metamorphosis' of some sort. I now have a wholly different attitude towards others."

Generating a joy-filled spirit is surely one of the great challenges of inspiring leader-managers.

9. SOW HARMONY

The Greek word for a pipe organ is *armonio*, an instrument in which each of the pipes is designed to play in harmony with the others. A harmonious organization is one in which inspiring leader-managers are able to encourage their associates to play or work in an atmosphere of sharing, giving selfless love. According to John Maxwell, the success of winning athletic teams can be traced to two major factors:

1. Strong leadership among coaches and players.
2. Harmonious relationships among the players (Maxwell 1995, 135–48).

Inspiring leader-managers of voluntary organizations go one step further than coaches of athletic teams by generating a spiritual harmony among associates at all levels.

In November, 1946, as a twenty-one-year-old volunteer, I deliberated spending my life at the Farm School, but was concerned that the School lacked an adequate financial base. When I expressed my reservation to the ninety-six-year-old widow of the founder, commonly referred to as "Mother House," she replied with a glimmer in her eyes, "Oh, my young friend, that School is God's work, and He'll see to it that it continues."

What did she mean by "He'll see to it that it continues?" It was not buildings, programs, equipment, or even money. It was a spirit of harmony among the staff that she and her husband had begun to sow forty years earlier. Even today, the School continues to reflect the intangible spirit inspired by the

House family. Three spouses of School Directors, her successors, have kept this spirit alive by walking in the footsteps of that spirit person, "Mother House." It was not so much what she said, but what she did that brought that harmony into the life of the School.

A pipe organ, by itself, is not enough to produce harmony. It needs the compositions of a Johann Sebastian Bach and organists like Albert Schweitzer to create inspiring music. Working together, inspiring leader-managers at all levels sow the true harmony that fills a concert hall or an organization with that extra dimension. It is often referred to at the Farm School as the "Spirit of Dr. House"—the harmony of communicating hearts.

10. CULTIVATE OPTIMISM

Exuberant optimism is the quality that made Theo Litsas, Associate Director of the American Farm School, an inspiring leader-manager (Draper 1994). On the day after the occupying forces had blown up the Farm School's classroom building toward the end of World War II, he was already looking forward to rebuilding a better structure more suited to expanding enrollment. In the next breath he was expressing gratitude that they had not blown up all the buildings! Five years later, communist guerrillas kidnapped the whole senior class, forty-three boys. On the following day Litsas was assuring their parents that their sons would escape and return, which they did—in time to graduate!

People who knew Theo well often discussed the source of his spiritual strength that he passed on to associates. He had been brought up as a Greek Orthodox in Turkey. He was obviously influenced by the Sufi tradition, the mystics of the Moslem faith of which the Hodja stories are such an integral part. Early on in his professional career he worked closely with the British Quakers who had a profound impact on him. During his years at the Farm School he gained great inspiration from the whole House family, and particularly "Mother House." Every activity of his life seemed to become a work of love inspired by the variety of spiritual values from his early years.

He had a way of welcoming each new visitor and each new day with a sense of optimism about what the day would bring. Possibly his name, Theodore (*Theos*-God's—*doro*-gift) prompted his outlook in his early life. He somehow sensed that what he did would nurture those with whom he was associated.

Nico Papaconstantinou was a senior at the Farm School in 1957 when he was diagnosed as having tuberculosis and given a ten-month sick leave. The doctors predicted little hope for recovery. He wrote:

> "Theodore Litsas called me to his office and said, 'The doctor told me your condition is serious, but I am sure you will recover in a couple of months.' To my surprise (and the doctors') the wound in my lung was cured in two months. When he said 'in a couple of months,' he wanted to give me courage, and deep inside he wished it to happen! From that moment on I was convinced. When the doctor told me the good news, I replied, '**I KNEW IT**!' It was amazing how easily he transferred his optimism to me."[6]

Today Nico has Theo's position in charge of student activities—sharing Theo's optimism with students at the Farm School forty years later.

All those who remember Theo recall his exuberant joy and optimism that made him such an outstanding inspiring leader-manager. He saw himself as an instrument of love and sharing from deep in his heart. He had a capacity to inspire this love in others and encourage them in turn to pass it on. He saw his life at the School as a path that led him to something greater than he could envision alone. Out of his love and reverence for the spirit person within, he seized every opportunity to share his exuberance, joy, and optimism with others, sensing that deep inside there was a strength greater than himself.

Hardly a day would pass in the life of the Farm School when Theo's optimism would not rub off on another individual whose life he touched. His energy and understanding expressed by his personal involvement in others may best be expressed by a few thoughts adapted from *Rugby Chapel* by Matthew Arnold. They should be a challenge to inspiring leader-managers at all levels.[7]

> "You alight in our organization!
> At your voice,
> Panic, despair, flee away,
> You move through the ranks, recall
> The stragglers, refresh the outworn,
> Praise, re-inspire the brave!
> Order and courage return."

11. REACH OUT

At the Farm School, the process of generating a sense of compassion is referred to as "Reaching Out," based on a book with this title by the late Henri Nouwen (1975).[8] According to this concept there are three aspects of people's lives:

1. their feelings about their inner self,
2. those about their fellow human beings, and
3. those that relate to their spiritual selves.

Inspiring leader-managers think of themselves in relation to all three levels of their being. This can be observed as they apply Nouwen's philosophy.

1. Move from *loneliness* to *solitude*. In their relationship with themselves, inspiring leader-managers reach out from a sense of isolation, whether alone or in a group, to a feeling of solitude, that inner peace that many experience regardless of external circumstances. Leader-managers, who appear indifferent or too busy to care, generate a sense of loneliness. Those who nurture concern and warmth inculcate a satisfying feeling in solitude among associates.

2. Reach out from *hostility* to *hospitality*. When first meeting new associates, many managers unconsciously exhibit a sense of hostility, making others feel threatened or uncomfortable. Inspiring leader-managers have a way of making everyone with whom they associate feel warmly welcomed and at home.

3. Transfer preoccupation from *material possessions* to *spiritual values*. Managers often attach greater importance to buildings, furnishings, or organizational structure. Inspiring leader-managers reach out beyond material possessions. They compassionately help associates develop self-confidence and positive self-esteem, while, at the same time, guiding them in their own search for the spiritual being within themselves.

Many customers arrive at an organization's front door with empty bags seeking to fill them with the organization's spirit; others come with half-filled bags marked "FRAGILE—don't knock me or I might break"; others come with bags so full they only want to unload them. The latter have no real interest in absorbing anything from their new environment. Inspiring leader-managers reach out to all their associates, help them identify their needs, and discover ways in which their organization can meet these needs, particularly on a spiritual level.

12. LET YOUR LIGHT SHINE

Inspiring leader-managers have one thing in common—they have all lived through Abraham Maslow's *peak experience,*

> the moment of "great joy, the ecstasy,
> the vision of another world,
> or another level of living" (Maslow 1971, 170).

They carry their peak experiences one step further, feeling compelled to share these experiences with others.

Peak experiences can grow out of a variety of circumstances: watching a sunrise in the Himalayas or a sunset over Mount Olympus across the Aegean; singing Handel's *Messiah* as part of a five-hundred-voice chorus; sitting on a cliff overlooking the sea as the full moon rises across the waters; listening to Beethoven's Ninth Symphony conducted by Leonard Bernstein; studying differential equations under an inspired mathematics teacher who sees beauty in his formulas; sharing the experience of a creative scientist who is on the threshold of a new discovery; living in that ecstatic moment of childbirth as a woman, an experience no man may share; walking barefoot on a mountain path, knowing you are walking on Holy Ground.

Inspiring leader-managers carry their peak experiences a step further. They seek to recreate them for others, to raise the experience of their associates and customers to new levels of the sacred. Candle-lighting services are a common component of many religions of the world, seeking to recreate the peak experience of their traditional spirituality.

One of the most impressive is the Easter Resurrection Service of the Greek Orthodox Church. Shortly before midnight, the lights are extinguished in the church so that all is in darkness except for one small flame over the holy table. As midnight approaches, the priest lights his candle from the single flame and shares the light with the elders. They in turn light the candles which individual members of the congregation have brought with them. As the candlelight spreads in waves, it illumines the whole church, inspiring a spirit of warmth and unity among the parishioners. At the end of the service, they carry their lighted candles home to light the lamp before the sacred icon in that holy corner they have designated as the family shrine.

Inspiring leader-managers endeavor to create such experiences for their associates through which they, too, may relive earlier peak experiences or discover new ones. When I was installed as the third director of the American Farm School in Greece on May 29, 1955, my brother, Parker, sent Tad and me a telegram from the United States that read, "Matthew 5:16." This reading from the New Testament is probably the greatest challenge of all for inspiring leader-managers:

> "Let your light so shine before men that they may see your good works and glorify your Father which is in heaven."

Leaders and managers, not concerned with the spiritual aspect of their organization, can effectively achieve their goals without striving for this additional dimension in their work. Inspiring leader-managers add an extra challenge to their life's dream—to inspire others as they have been inspired. Theirs may be a difficult goal to attain, but like Cavafy's *ITHAKA,* it is, after all, the journey, and not the destination which counts!

TABLE 10.1 Self-Evaluation Form

CHAPTER 10: BECOME AN INSPIRING LEADER-MANAGER						
Where are you as a leader-manager on the scale: *Kakomiris* (1) . . . to . . . *Nikokiris* (5)?						
TOPIC	1	2	3	4	5	PRIORITY
1. Radiates inner peace (page 120)						
2. Communicates as a listener (page 120)						
3. Reflects sincerity (page 121)						
4. Challenges spirits to soar (page 121)						
5. Inspires self-confidence (page 122)						
6. Commits self to others (page 123)						
7. Enthuses associates (page 123)						
8. Generates a joyful spirit (page 123)						
9. Sows harmony (page 124)						
10. Cultivates optimism (page 125)						
11. Reaches out (page 126)						
12. Reflects an internal light (page 127)						

(Numbers in parentheses refer to pages where subject is mentioned.)

1. For each topic, place an "X" under the 1, 2, 3, 4, or 5 to show where you think you are now as a leader-manager.
2. For each topic, place a "Y" under the 1, 2, 3, 4, or 5 to show where you would like to be.
3. Mark any item where the topic does not apply to your program "NA" (Not Applicable).
4. Under priority, enter a number on a scale from 5 (top priority) to 1 (lowest priority).
5. Identify three or four of your primary concerns on this theme and develop a "POLKA" plan of work to deal with them.
6. List other concerns, share them with your associates, and evaluate them as above.

NOTES

1. Notes from the diary of Robert J. Rawson, who visited the American Farm School in 1920. The original notes are available in the School Archives.

2. Oldham (Third Month, Day 3) speaks of sincerity as one of the great virtues which apply to leader-managers. He quotes Thomas Carlyle, *Heroes and Hero-Worship*, and William James, *Varieties of Religious Experience*.

3. Oldham (First Month, Day 23) emphasizes the challenge and reward of vicissitudes in life, particularly for inspired individuals. He finds great support for his convictions in quoting Nietzshe, *Gotzendommerung*.

4. Talk by Constantine Markopoulos, Director of Vocational Education, Greek Ministry of Education, to the students of the American Farm School, 1988.

5. Oldham (Second Month, Day 25) quotes Robert Louis Stevenson in *Across the Plains* and St. Francis of Assisi in *The Mirror of Perfection*.

6. Letter to the author from Nico Papaconstantinou, June, 1999.

7. Oldham (First Month, Day 5). Paraphrased from Matthew Arnold, *Rugby Chapel*.

8. *Reaching Out—The Three Movements of the Spiritual Life* (New York: Doubleday, 1975). This is a book which everyone aspiring to become an inspiring leader-manager should read and re-read from time to time.

ITHAKA

C. P. CAVAFY'S METAPHORICAL CHALLENGE TO INSPIRING LEADER-MANAGERS

As you set out for Ithaka

hope the voyage is a long one,

full of adventure, full of discovery.

Laistrygonians and Cyclops,

angry Poseidon—don't be afraid of them:

you'll never find things like that on your way

as long as you keep your thoughts raised high,

as long as a rare excitement

stirs your spirit and your body.

Laistrygonians and Cyclops,

wild Poseidon—you won't encounter them

unless you bring them along inside your soul,

unless your soul sets them up in front of you.

Hope the voyage is a long one.

May there be many a summer morning when,

with what pleasure, what joy,

you come into harbors seen for the first time;

may you stop at Phoenician trading stations

to buy fine things,

mother of pearl and coral, amber and ebony,

sensual perfume of every kind—

as many sensual perfumes as you can;

and may you visit many Egyptian cities

to gather stores of knowledge from their scholars.

Keep Ithaka always in your mind.

Arriving there is what you are destined for.

But do not hurry the journey at all.

Better if it lasts for years,

so you are old by the time you reach the island,

wealthy with all you have gained on the way,

not expecting Ithaka to make you rich.

Ithaka gave you the marvelous journey.

Without her you would not have set out.

She has nothing left to give you now.

And if you find her poor, Ithaka won't have fooled you.

Wise as you will have become, so full of experience,

you will have understood by then what these Ithakas mean.

THREE CASE STUDIES

INVOLVING SERVICE ORGANIZATIONS

BASED ON EXPERIENCES BY THE AMERICAN FARM SCHOOL
THESSALONIKI, GREECE

The case studies that follow are based on a number of planning experiences that were related to the American Farm School. They either involved the School directly or where the School acted as a catalyst working with a variety of private, proprietary, and government organizations. They are totally unrelated to each other, but reflect the extent of the School's activities.

The first case study describes a Community Development Program in the Prefecture (County) of Thessaloniki working with 151 villages. The program was initiated in 1958 with a grant of C$10,000 from the Unitarian Service Committee of Canada and came to an unfortunate end in 1967 when the country was taken over by a dictatorial junta which had little confidence in democratic approaches to participatory development.

The second case study involves the American Farm School during a particularly turbulent period in its history between 1974 and 1978. The problems grew out of a growing lack of confidence among some of the Board of Trustees in the United States as well as a sense of disillusionment among many of the staff. This took place during a period of strong anti-American sentiment in Greece following the junta. At the same time there were significant changes in Greek legislation which necessitated radical changes in the curriculum and the age level of the students.

The third case study describes a rather innovative approach to introducing new systems of education in Albania. These programs included secondary agricultural education, adult education through short courses, and training programs in education at the Agricultural University of Tirana.

These three studies should prove helpful to those interested in the planning process as it relates to a variety of program activities of service organizations.

CASE STUDY I

PLANNING BY COMMUNITY DEVELOPMENT

CONCEPTUALIZE THE NEED

Chambers proposes that "it is often best to start, to do something, to learn from doing" (Chambers 1983, 217). This is an approach quite different from the concept of strategic planning. This case study begins with one of the most successful programs undertaken by the American Farm School. In recognition of this contribution the School was awarded the highest decoration accorded by the Greek government to a foreign organization.

The American Farm School's involvement in community development began late one night in my office with Associate Director Theo Litsas. He had just returned from refereeing a battle between a director of a public school and the president of a community a few kilometers from the Farm School. "Isn't it sad," Litsas mused, "that the only time we can convince these community leaders to communicate is when they have a fight."

Within two hours we had conceived a "let's learn from doing" scheme. "Why not organize community development committees in a small cluster of communities and find out whether they would be willing or able to meet periodically to discuss their communities' problems and seek possible solutions?" It sounded like a good idea, but there was still a major first step to be taken.

SEEK COMMUNITY WISDOM

When Charles House retired after thirty-seven years as Director of the Farm School, his last words of advice to me, his twenty-nine-year-old successor, reflected years of practical experience. "If you have a new idea you wish to implement, do not go to the high officials in the government or the university professors. Go out among the people in local neighborhoods. In every community you will find a few individuals who may not have much education, but have within them the wisdom of the ages." Litsas and I spent the better part of our free evenings over the next two months in coffee shops lit by gas-lamps or community council offices discussing this idea and seeking local advice. There were three reactions in the local communities.

1. It was a great idea that, in fact, once existed during four-hundred years of Turkish occupation. The concept was therefore not foreign to them.

2. There was little the local leaders could accomplish if they could not gain the support of (and at the same time avoid the interference of) local-level government officials. These officials appeared to control every aspect of community life.

3. The best advice they could obtain would come from other neighboring village leaders—if they could have a chance of exchanging experiences and accomplishments with them.

IDENTIFY THEIR PROBLEMS AS THEY SEE THEM

Up until this point, the School had been in Röling's DO TO and DO FOR mode (Röling 1988). It was the School's own idea that we were planning to implement based on our felt needs. From the very beginning the administration was determined that the only financial contribution the School would make to such a program was to:

1. employ a Community Development Coordinator,
2. provide him with a motorbike, and
3. host the Community Development Conferences.

The role of the coordinator would be to work with the community leaders on *their* problems based on how *they* saw them. (As the number of conferences and distance from the Farm School increased, the meetings were held in coffee shops, schools, or public buildings.)

ORGANIZE THE LEADERS

The first step in the program was for each community to form community development committees. These committees consisted of elected and informal leaders who were chosen by the citizens themselves. Soon after the program began, they discovered that no women had been included in the committees—an oversight that was quickly corrected!

GENERATE SUPPORT FROM THE TOP

The next step was to organize a voluntary prefecture-level, community development committee made up of key officials associated with the local areas, including the directors of public works, agriculture, the agricultural bank, the veterinary service, welfare, tourism and education, and the local bishop. This group spent considerable time planning a three-day conference, for fifteen to twenty leaders from each of six communities. The speakers at the conference who were members of the prefecture development committee were given fifteen minutes to speak on the question, "What can you do to develop your community in my specialty and how can we help you?"

INSIST ON LOCAL-LEVEL PARTICIPATION

The fifteen-minute presentation was followed by "time for questions" and discussion time for village representatives to make sure that the speakers had not been too theoretical. After each group of speakers in one area of interest, such as agriculture, education, or public works had finished, the gathering broke up into local community groups, which discussed the projects presented by the officials or other community members. During these group discussions they decided which projects were appropriate for their own community and when and how they could be implemented. Not surprisingly, because of their enthusiasm, they tended to be overly optimistic about what they could accomplish.

COMMUNITY-DESIGNED SOLUTIONS

On the final day, the representatives of each community were asked to report to the conference on their plans for the coming year—a very exciting moment for all of them. Even though they obviously could not accomplish everything, they were encouraged to start on small projects. They realized that they would have a difficult time when they returned home because their fellow villagers would not initially share their enthusiasm.

TRAIN THE PARTICIPANTS TO BECOME LEADER-MANAGERS

They were urged to set up a similar conference at the neighborhood or community level in which each of the conferees from the villages would take the role of one of the speakers at the conference to convey their enthusiasm to their neighbors. By this time the Thessaloniki Community Development Program had turned into a DO WITH program coordinated by Dr. A. E. Trimis (1967) working in cooperation with the Thessaloniki Prefect and his staff.

LET THEM MANAGE THE IMPLEMENTATION

Many local citizens were convinced that nothing would be done. Although some of the speakers were pessimistic, they were willing to try. At the end of the first year, the prefecture committee discovered that even though the communities had not implemented all the programs to which they were committed, they had accomplished a great deal and had established communication among themselves and with the officials.

ASSURE COMMUNICATIONS AMONG ALL LEVELS

Most committees had met once a month as agreed. The civil servants and local leaders had changed their attitude toward each other. When extra money was needed from a government source, the officials involved, who had developed a much closer tie with these community leaders, were somehow able to find it. Even such complex tasks as new roads, water supply systems, and new schoolhouses were completed. At the time this program was being organized at the local level, an effort was made by the Greek National Foundation (a Greek NGO) and the Ministry of the Interior to form similar prefecture level community development committees in each prefecture and at the national level.

BEWARE OF AUTHORITARIAN APPROACHES

About ten years later, a government that believed in the authoritarian approach to solving community problems came into power and appointed its own officials, who ended the program. Until then, many of the communities had continued their planning meetings and implemented a variety of projects. The new government, like all dictatorships, was based on the premise that development depends on what the national authorities can DO TO and DO FOR local communities and that the thought of accomplishing anything with a DO WITH philosophy is so much "liberal wishful thinking!" Conversely, their authoritarian attitude was conducive to building better roads and assuring that trains run on time, but had little impact on cultivating initiative among the citizens.

LEARN FROM THE VILLAGERS

Twenty-five years after the Thessaloniki Community Development Program was started, community leaders continued to speak enthusiastically about their accomplishments. Roads, churches, water works, and schoolhouses built during that time are visible proof of its results. The trees planted then have grown into community-owned forests. More importantly, many of the leaders of that time learned to work together for the benefit of their community. "Is local community planning possible?" the Farm School was asked when it started its program. Community members and their leaders as well as government officials working together proved that it definitely is possible.

OBSERVATIONS ON THE COMMUNITY DEVELOPMENT APPROACH

Several years later, a small group of the original participants among the prefecture officials gathered to reflect on the value of the community development approach to the development process. The success of similar urban and rural development programs has demonstrated the validity of this approach. The key to this success rests on individuals such as Tony Trimis and other inspired leader-managers of community development programs who win the total confidence of village and government officials.

It might be useful to summarize some of their observations:

1. People we seek to help can teach us how to plan our help.

2. Villagers often learn more from each other about planning than from us as outsiders.

3. New programs have to "fit in" to prevalent social and organizational structures.

4. Planning new programs must incorporate, build on, and take advantage of the strengths of existing plans and programs.

5. There is synergistic value in bringing people together to share experiences and dreams in the planning process.

6. Those we seek to help must have a sense of ownership in the plans they develop. *Our* plans must become *their* plans and *their* plans, *ours*.

7. By becoming "salesmen" of plans (which they think of as their own) villagers understand them better, grow more committed to them, and sustain them as their own.

8. To the extent that our plan helps them to deal with *their* felt needs, to that degree will the program acquire momentum as their plan.

9. A development worker's role is to help village leaders identify problems that are important to the local citizens who must articulate solutions as their own plans.

10. Activities vertically and horizontally integrated in the fabric of a society will be assured of lasting momentum.

11. This momentum will be maintained as exogenous leaders are replaced by indigenous leaders. The status of the local leaders is enhanced by their own successes.

12. No foreigner will be any more effective than the indigenous leadership through which he chooses to work.

Humor is the best lubricant for overcoming friction in community development!

CASE STUDY II

IMPROVING ORGANIZATIONAL PLANNING

The second case study uses a stormy period in the Farm School's history to illustrate the importance of strategic planning for voluntary organizations and the various steps required for effective planning. (The concept of strategic planning seems more appropriate for educational institutions inasmuch as most of the faculty and administrators implementing them have a clear understanding of the implications of the term.) Such plans grow out of a clear understanding of an institution's mission, which gives it direction. However, the plans must be specific and clarify priorities and deadlines.

ENSURE CONTINUAL REVIEW

In addition to long-range planning, institutions, individual departments, and staff members must have clearly defined medium-term and short-term goals through which to evaluate their progress. Key to this process is a continual review (at least once every year) of the goals of an organization and the methods it is applying to implement them.

Organizations do not operate in a vacuum. They are an integral part of an ever-changing external and internal environment. Demands and expectations of quality in an organization are constantly in a state of flux. Failure to adapt to these changes can easily result in an organization's decline and eventual demise.

DEFINE OBJECTIVES CLEARLY

The Farm School's recovery from a period of considerable difficulty in its history demonstrates the importance of careful planning. The School's problems became acute in the 1970s, when the Greek government completely revised educational programs and required the Farm School to follow suit. During this period, enrollment dropped by two-thirds and the cost per student more than doubled. Staff members became demoralized, Trustees grew disillusioned, and students wondered about their future. My failure as Director to provide adequate leadership exacerbated the problems of the School. The faculty and Trustees were eagerly seeking clearly stated objectives that could adapt to changing needs.

INSTIGATE PARTICIPATORY PLANNING

I also fell short in my effort to instigate a program of participatory planning which would have included Trustees, faculty, administration, and farm and maintenance staff as well as the alumni and students in a participatory management approach. The School wanted to train village youth and adults as well as to operate a demonstration farm, but beyond these points there seemed to be little agreement on the School's mission and its long-term goals or their implementation. Like Hodja, we might have said, "We think it is us, the American Farm School, if God is willing."

CLARIFY PROCEDURES FOR EFFECTIVE PLANNING

John Henry House clearly stated his goals in the School's Charter of Incorporation: "Providing agricultural and industrial training under Christian supervision for youth . . . in order that they may be trained to appreciate the dignity of manual labor, and be helped to lives of self-respect, thrift, and industry." Seventy years later, the School's activities and programs had grown too numerous and complex to be defined by such a simple statement. As efforts to resolve the conflict continued, three procedures to provide more effective planning were agreed upon:

1. A clear mission statement.
2. A participatory survey by an outside expert.
3. A long-term view prepared in a participatory fashion by management.

SEEK A CLEAR MISSION STATEMENT

During the discussions, among Board members, staff, and others about the future direction of the Farm School in 1978, the Chairman, the administration, and a faculty committee drafted a statement that attempted to summarize where they felt the School should be going. A Board committee reviewed and further modified it. It was finally brought before the whole Board during a two-day meeting devoted to long-range planning and goal clarification.

This mission statement was adopted after lengthy discussions. The staff looked upon this statement as a broad guideline rather than as a basis for scrutinizing specific activities and programs. The administration and faculty restructured it in outline form to give precise guidance on programs. The simplified form made it easier to clarify which activities were most important. The Trustees felt that this approach would provide overall policy direction to the School.

RELATE MISSION TO PROGRAM-ORIENTED PLANNING

While the mission statement was being developed, the Board commissioned Professor Irwin Sanders, a sociologist and leading authority on rural Greece, to study the objectives of the School in view of the rapid changes in the villages. After interviewing Trustees, faculty, officials, alumni, and villagers, Dr. Sanders took an approach different from the Board in his report. Rather than preparing a broad mission statement that might be confusing, he made his recommendations in terms of specific program goals and activities.

STAGE IMPLEMENTATION

Dr. Sanders then prepared a time frame for staging his recommendations, which provided both priorities and deadlines. The Sanders report concluded:

> "Since it is impossible to meet all of the challenges confronting the School at this time, it seems best to deal with them in stages, or in sequence. Staging means that at a given time we will seek to upgrade one program while putting other programs on 'hold.'
>
> Administrative and staff time is so limited that to diffuse it too widely is self-defeating. An agreement upon program staging can make possible long-term budgeting and some predictable allocation of resources over the next three, four or five years."

The Sanders report became an invaluable guide to the staff in planning activities on an annual basis. The Board of Trustees decided to review the whole study every few years in order to evaluate achievements and to provide future guidelines.

INVOLVE THE POLICYMAKERS

In addition to clarifying the School's goals, an invaluable byproduct of these studies was the personal involvement of the Trustees and members of the faculty in the planning process. As a result of the meetings and informal discussions, the Trustees developed a better understanding of each other as well as gaining a deeper insight into the function of the School and its programs. The most useful contribution of the whole undertaking proved to be faculty and volunteer participation. What had originally been a near calamity for the School turned into the focal point of a new spirit of cooperation among faculty, Trustees, and friends.

The most effective way to maintain the interest of trustees is to seek their advice in the planning process, even though this approach may sometimes seem time consuming and frustrating. The same principle applies to organizations that are supervised by government departments or committees of management. It is vitally important to maintain the involvement of those who establish policy. It has been said of involved trustees (Davis 1957):

"More to be desired are they than gold."

INCLUDE THE STAFF IN PLANNING

Individual members of the staff feel personally committed to the success of the long-range plan only to the extent that they shared in preparing the recommendations for it. It is better to avoid consulting them entirely than to seek their advice and not allow them to share in the final decision-making process. Over the years, some of the richest sources of innovative ideas for the School have not only been faculty members but also laborers and technicians, many of whom grew up in the villages. A large number of graduates employed by the School have played an invaluable role in the planning process. Administrators should never underestimate the potential contribution of peasant wisdom in developing long-term goals.

SEEK CLIENT PARTICIPATION

Other groups that can make important contributions to the planning process are the students themselves, adult trainees from the communities, and leaders from area industries. These individuals are an organization's key clients and reflect customer expectations. In forming local advisory committees, organizations should select members who represent interests associated with their clients. In the case of the American Farm School, they include representatives from agribusiness, the local agricultural office, home economics department, district cooperative office, the local university, credit union and bank, as well as representative organizations, community leaders, housewives, and alumni.

CASE STUDY III

CROSS-CULTURAL "DO WITH" PLANNING

THE ALBANIAN EXPERIENCE

The experience of the American Farm School working with the Albanian Ministries of Education (MOE) and Agriculture (MOAF) and the Agricultural University of Tirana (AUT) in the decade of the 1990s is another useful case study of participatory planning and development in the DO WITH mode. It began with a decision by Oregon State University to participate in a needs-assessment survey at AUT shortly following the fall of the communist regime.

During the study, the American Farm School participants on the team were invited by the Ministry of Education to visit one of their somewhat run-down secondary vocational agricultural schools that had been operated by the Hoxha regime for almost fifty years. The MOE staff was eager to discover how the American Farm School might help them adapt new programs based on the Greek experience. They were talking of reorganizing twenty such schools, beginning with six pilot projects.

PREPARE AN OVERALL PLAN

The MOE officials and the representatives from Greece agreed on a three-step plan. There were three elements that were clear at this point:

1. They had to visit Greece to see the American Farm School's programs in action—what was referred to as the finished picture of the puzzle—and decide which parts of the puzzle they wanted to implement in their Albanian schools.

2. Funds were needed to cover the initial costs.

3. It was evident that there was what John Dewey (1910) referred to as "learning readiness" on the part of the MOE officials and among the staff at the schools where they wanted to work.

The representatives from Greece made it clear from the beginning that their role would be that of a "midwife." The schools were "Albanian babies" and the Albanians would have to give birth to them.

TRAIN THE LEADER-MANAGERS

As the MOE plans (and those of the visitors, too) were much too vague at this point, it was virtually impossible to formulate any kind of a long-term plan, especially since it had to be *their* plan. The American Farm School was fortunate in finding limited funds from a Greek foundation and a Greek semi-government agency for "seed money." The funds were designated:

1. For travel by key Albanian officials and staff to Greece to organize two seminars at the American Farm School,

2. To finance three Farm School retirees to visit Albania to prepare a needs assessment survey.

By the end of their Greek visit, the Albanian representatives had seen a picture of the completed puzzle which they were trying to assemble. As a small informal group of Albanians, Greeks, and Americans, these key individuals were able to agree on where they wanted to go and how they would get there. From the very beginning, the Albanian counterparts were the inspired leader-managers of the whole program.

DRAFT A DETAILED PROGRAM PLAN

Three members of the group, two Albanian MOE staff and I, locked ourselves in an MOE office for several hours and drafted a twelve-point agreement which was signed by the Ministers of Education and Agriculture and the AUT Rector. It provided for the reorganization of two pilot schools and a new Department of Vocational Agricultural and Extension Education at AUT.

Key to the whole process was the formation of a committee with the incredible acronym of CCVATA (Coordinating Committee for Vocational Agricultural Training in Albania) whose function it was to coordinate the activities of some ten different organizations that had a part in the program. The overall program was identified by the acronym AVATAR (Alliance for Vocational Agricultural Training in the Albanian Region).

ORGANIZE A COORDINATING COMMITTEE

A vital role of the CCVATA involved assuring communication among the various national and international organizations working on the project. Within Albania it was important for the CCVATA to maintain close contact between the central government, AUT, and the two pilot schools and local municipal authorities in their districts and potential parents and students.

TRAIN THE TRAINERS AS INSPIRED LEADER-MANAGERS

At the international level it was not only important to train the instructors at the schools, but to train the trainers of extension agents and vocational agricultural teachers at the AUT. An American Farm School coordinator undertook to recruit the professional staff who could provide the instruction both in Albania, Greece, and eventually in Northern Ireland. The United States NGO, Volunteers in Overseas Cooperative Assistance (VOCA), recruited volunteers who would conduct the courses and seminars at all three levels.

SEEK FINANCIAL SUPPORT

It was a strictly "hand-to-mouth" operation from a financial point of view. Special help was provided by the Albanian Ministries of Education and Agriculture, European Union special funds, Greek government allocations, and many thousands of hours of voluntary assistance from Albanian, Greek, United Kingdom, and United States individuals and groups.

IMPLEMENT THE PLAN

Within a year of the signing of the CCVATA Agreement, the two schools had been renovated, textbooks and lab manuals written and translated, and teachers trained. This made it possible to enroll more than 250 students in the two courses. Three years after the Agreement was signed, 130 graduates, boys and girls, stood before their proud parents, from the communities surrounding the two schools, to receive their diplomas.

TRAIN LEADER-MANAGERS FOR THE "LONG HAUL"

Five years after the training effort was undertaken, the MOE recognized that it was in a position to coordinate the training activities at the agricultural schools on its own. In a real sense, the babies had been born, and there was no future place for the midwife. From a long-range point of view there continued to be a need for assistance in organizing a Department for the Preparation of Agricultural Vocational Teachers and Extension Agents (DPAVTEA) at the AUT.

This new Department served the secondary agricultural schools by training future staff for the long term as well as agricultural extension agents for the newly established Extension Service of the Ministry of Agriculture and Food. Primary emphasis in these courses at both the undergraduate and graduate level was in teaching methods and communications as well as vocational training for village youths in agricultural skills.

ORGANIZE JOINT PLANNING LOCALLY

There were many elements that contributed to the success of this program, but the key was in joint planning under the leadership of the MOE. There were continual reports from the village level about their needs, ambitions and dreams, through the staff of the schools, to the Ministries of Education and Agriculture and the Faculty of the AUT. An extended group of international volunteers avoided a DO TO or DO FOR approach. The expatriates saw their role as DO WITH their Albanian associates. The original program has been expanded to include six schools as well as an additional higher level of senior high school vocational training in response to the appeals of the students and their parents. Despite a variety of problems, a true sense of pride has grown among those involved through their joint efforts (Mykerezi 1996).

The concept of the POLKA has played a key role in implementing the new programs. It was necessary to have the PLAN, but it was also vital to be able to ADJUST, to maintain the flexibility needed to adapt the plan to the needs and aspirations of the clients—the village families and their children. Who deserves the real credit? There is a simple answer in a saying heard in Greece, a vital lesson for any leader-manager:

> **THERE IS NO LIMIT TO WHAT YOU CAN ACCOMPLISH IF YOU DON'T CARE WHO GETS THE CREDIT.**

AMERICAN FARM SCHOOL CREED

I BELIEVE

in a permanent agriculture, a soil that grows richer, rather than poorer from year to year.

I BELIEVE

in living not for self but for others so that future generations may not suffer on account of my farming methods.

I BELIEVE

that tillers of the soil are stewards of the land and will be held accountable for the faithful performance of their trust.

I AM PROUD

to be a farmer and will try to be worthy of the name.

John Henry House
(circa 1910)

(Marder 1979)

BIBLIOGRAPHY

Alper Associates. 1992. "Understanding the Basic Concepts of TQM." Unpublished course outline. Jersey City, N.J.: C. William Alper Associates.

Benor, Daniel and James O. Harrison. 1977. *Agricultural Extension: The Training and Visit System*. Washington, D.C.: World Bank.

Borg, Marcus J. 1994. *Meeting Jesus Again for the First Time*. New York: HarperCollins Publishers.

Bullfinch's Mythology. 1979. New York: Avenel Books, Crown Publishers.

Burnham, Daniel H. 1970. *Make No Little Plans*. Printed by American Farm School Trustee, Ruth Wells, whose husband, George B. Wells, President and CEO of the American Optical Company, was a descendent of Burnham. Sturbridge, Mass.

Cavafy, C. P. 1975. *Collected Poems*. Translated by Edmund Keeley and Philip Sherrard. Edited by George Savidis. Princeton, N.J.: Princeton University Press.

Chambers, Robert. 1983. *Rural Development: Putting the Last First*. Harlow, Essex: Longman Scientific & Technical.

————, Arnold Pacey and Lori Ann Thrupp. 1989. *Farmer First, Farmer Innovation and Agricultural Research*. London: Intermediate Technology Publications.

Coonradt, Charles A. 1984. *The Game of Work*. Salt Lake City: Shadow Mountain Press.

Davis, Paul H. "All the World Stands Aside." In *Association of American Colleges Bulletin* 43, no. 2, May 1957.

Daily Word. Lee's Summit, Mo.: Unity School of Christianity, April 1997, August 1998.

Dewey, John. 1910. *How We Think*. New York: D.C. Heath and Company.

Draper, Charlotte Whitney. 1994. *The American Farm School of Thessaloniki, a Family Album*. Thessaloniki, Greece: American Farm School.

Drucker, Peter. 1968. *The Practice of Management*. London: Pan Books Limited.

————. 1990. *Managing the Non-Profit Organization*. New York: HarperCollins Publishers.

Eisen, Armand. 1995. Quoting Alphonse de Lamartine. *The Little Book of Angels*. Kansas City, Mo.: Andrews McMeel.

Eliade, Mircea. 1959. *The Sacred and the Profane, the Nature of Religion*. New York: Harcourt Brace Jovanovic.

Etling, Arlen. "Leadership for Nonformal Education." In *Journal of International Agricultural and Extension Education*, Spring 1994: 16–24.

Facino, Marsilio. 1980. *Facino Marsilio: The Book of Life*. Translated by Charles Boer. Dallas: Spring Publications.

Fromm, Erich. 1976. *To Have or To Be?* New York: A Bantam Book, Harper and Row Publishers, Inc.

Frost, Robert. 1971. *The Poetry of Robert Frost*. Edited by Edward Connery Lathem. Barre, Mass.: The Imprint Society, Inc.

Gabor, Andrea. 1990. *The Man Who Discovered Quality*. New York: Penguin Books.

Gavrilia, The Monastic and D. Gangakis. 1996. *The Ascetic of Love, the Monastic Gavrilia*. Athens: Eptalofos Press.

Gardner, John W. 1964. *Self Renewal. The Individual and the Innovative Society*. New York: Harper and Row.

Hanh, Thich Nhat. 1987. *Being Peace*. Berkeley, Calif.: Parallax Press.

Hammarskjold, Dag. 1964. *Markings*. New York: Alfred A. Knopf.

Heider, John. 1986. *The Tao of Leadership*. New York: Bantam Books.

Homer. 1996. *The Odyssey*. Translated by Robert Fagles. New York: Viking Penguin.

Kazantzakis, Nikos. 1946. *Zorba the Greek*. London: Faber and Faber.

Lansdale, David P. 1990. "Citadel Under Siege: The Contested Mission of an Evangelical Christian Liberal Arts College." Ph.D Dissertation, Stanford University, Stanford, Calif.

Lansdale, Bruce. 1986. *Master Farmer: Teaching Small Farmers Management*. Boulder, Colo.: Westview Press.

———. 1979. *METAMORPHOSIS, or, Why I Love Greece*. New Rochelle, N.Y.: Caratzas Brothers Publishers.

Leslie, Keith and Krishna Sob. 1990. "Participatory Development." *Bulletin of Save the Children/USA*. Katmandu, Nepal.

London, Fran. "Chuckle a Day" *Rochester Review* (Winter 1995–96). Rochester, N.Y.: University of Rochester.

Marder, Brenda L. 1979. *Stewards of the Land: The American Farm School and Modern Greece*. Boulder, Colo.: East European Quarterly. Distributed by Columbia University Press, New York.

Maslow, Abraham. 1971. *The Farther Reaches of Human Nature*. New York: Penguin Books.

Maxwell, John C. 1995. *Developing the Leaders Around You*. Nashville, Tenn.: Thomas Nelson Publishers.

———. 1993. *Developing the Leader Within You*. Nashville, Tenn.: Thomas Nelson Publishers.

Meredith, Martin. 1997. *Nelson Mandela, A Biography*. London: Penguin Books.

Mindess, Harvey. "A Sense of Humor." Adapted from his book *Laughter and Liberation. Saturday Review of Literature* (August 21, 1971).

Minoudis, Christos. Letter to former Director of the American Farm School. Thessaloniki, Greece: American Farm School Archives, February 25, 1998.

Moore, Thomas. 1994. *Care of the Soul*. New York: Harper Perennial.

Mykerezi, Pavli. 1996. "Secondary Agricultural Education in Albania." Korça Agricultural School, Korça, Albania.

Nouwen, Henri J. M. 1975. *Reaching Out—The Three Movements of the Spiritual Life*. New York: Doubleday.

———. 1972. *Thomas Merton: Contemplative Critic*. Notre Dame, Ind.: Fides Publishers, Inc.

———. 1982. *With Open Hands*. Notre Dame, Ind.: Ave Maria.

Oldham, J. H. 1959. *A Devotional Diary*. Twentieth Edition. London: SCM Press, [1925]

Panas, Jerold. 1981. *Leadership*. Unpublished circular. Chicago: Jerold Panas and Partners, Inc.

Peck, M. Scott. 1978. *The Road Less Traveled*. New York: Simon and Schuster.

Peters, Tom. 1988. *Thriving on Chaos: Handbook for a Management Revolution*. New York: Knopf.

Pickering, John. 1848. *Ellino-agliko leksiko* (Greek-English Dictionary). Boston. (Privately reprinted in 1990 by Maria and Charalambos Vassilopoulos, Vassilopoulos Brothers, Athens.)

Pirsig, Robert M. 1979. *Zen and The Art of Motorcycle Maintenance*. New York: William Morrow and Company, Inc.

Platonis Opera, Tetralogias III–IV, OXIONI. John Burnet, ed. 1901. Cambridge: Cambridge University Press.

Röling, Niels. 1988. *Extension Science*. Cambridge: Cambridge University Press.

Schumacher, E. F. 1973. *Small Is Beautiful, Economics as if People Mattered*. Paperback Edition. London: Perennial Library, Harper and Row.

Schweitzer, Albert. 1959. "Civilization and Ethics." Quoted by Oldham, J. H. *A Devotional Diary*. London: SCM Press.

———. 1949. *Out of My Life and Thought*. New York: Henry Holt and Company.

Speerings, News and Information for Management. 1987. Palo Alto, Calif.: Syntex Labs, Inc.

Steindl-Rast, David. 1984. *Gratefulness, The Heart of Prayer*. Ramsey, N.J.: Paulist Press.

———. 1994. *A Listening Heart*. New York: Crossroad Publishing Company.

Thurman, Howard. 1953. *Meditations of the Heart*. New York: Harper and Row Publishers Inc.

Trimis, Antonios. 1967. *Community Development as an Element in Area and Regional Socio-economic Growth and Development*. Bozeman, Mont.: Montana State University. Ph.D. Dissertation. June.

Walton, Mary. 1986. *The Deming Management Method*. New York: The Putnam Publishing Group.

Williams, Richard L. 1994. *Essentials of Total Quality Management*. New York: amacon, American Management Association.

A BIBLIOGRAPHY OF HODJA STORIES

Ali Birand, Mehmet. *Stories of Hodja*. Istanbul.

Caplan, Leslie. 1973. *Tales of Goha*. London: Heinemann Educational Books Ltd.

Downing, Charles. 1964. *Tales of the Hodja*. London: Oxford University Press.

Gigliesi, Primerose and Robert C. Friend. 1982. *The Effendi and the Pregnant Pot, Uygur Folktales from China*. Beijing: New World Press.

Her Hakki Mahfuzdur. 1988. *202 Jokes of Nasreddin Hodja*. Istanbul: Galeri Minyatur—Tuncay Yurtsever.

Kabacali, Alpay. 1992. *Nasreddin Hodja*. Translated by Nüket Eraslan. Istanbul: Net Turistik Yayinlar.

Kelsey, Alice Geer. 1943. *Once the Hodja*. New York: Longmans, Green and Co.

Lansdale, Bruce. 1986. *Master Farmer: Teaching Small Farmers Management*. Boulder, Colo.: Westview Press.

Mayiopoulos, Stelios. 1965. *O Nasrettin Xotzas*. Athens: Bibliopoleion tis "Estias."

Shah, Idries. 1966. *The Exploits of the Incredible Mulla Nasrudin*. New York: Simon and Schuster.

———. 1968. *The Pleasantries of the Incredible Mulla Nasrudin*. London: Jonathan Cape.

——— and Richard Williams. 1973. *Once the Mullah—The Subtleties of the Inimitable Mulla Nasrudin*. London: Jonathan Cape.

Soloviof, Leonida. 1980. *O Nasredin Xotzas*. Athens: Dorikos.

Walker, Barbara. 1991. *Watermelons, Walnuts and the Wisdom of Allah, and Other Tales of the Hoca*. Lubbock, Texas: Texas Tech University Press.

Yagan, Turgay. n. d. *Stories of the Hodja*. Istanbul: Turgay Yagan, n. p.

ABOUT THE AUTHOR

Bruce Lansdale began his forty-three years at the American Farm School in Greece in 1947. Prior to that, he earned a Bachelor's Degree from the University of Rochester in Mechanical Engineering and subsequently a Master's Degree in Rural Sociology and Agricultural Education from Cornell. Under his leadership the Farm School became a multifaceted institution dedicated to quality "hands on" secondary education, cutting edge agricultural development, lifelong learning through short courses, and international training programs. Recognizing the contribution of these activities, the Greek government and the World Bank built an adult training center complete with lodging facilities on the Farm School campus.

His book, *Master Farmer*, has become a recognized tool in the developing world. He was awarded three successive Fulbright Grants as well as Rockefeller and Ford Foundation Fellowships and an honorary Ph.D. from the University of Thessaloniki. The Government of Greece has decorated him twice with the highest awards granted to foreign nationals.

Since his retirement in 1990, he and his wife, Tad, have been in demand as seminar leaders in Nepal, Albania, Bulgaria, Kosovo, Honduras, Malawi, Nigeria, India, and Tanzania.

Bruce has demonstrated the knack of being able to work effectively with people of various cultures where he uses his magical storytelling of Nasredin Hodja's exploits to make his points. In between their travels conducting seminars, the Lansdales live in Metamorphosis, Greece, in the summer and Santa Cruz, California, in the winter, often visiting their four children and eleven grandchildren.

GEORGE LAGAKIS

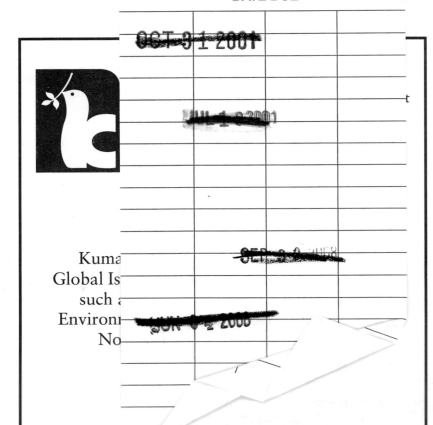

Kuma
Global Is
such a
Environr
No

To r HIGH a complimentary catalog or
to request writer's guidelines call or write:

Kumarian Press, Inc.
14 Oakwood Avenue
West Hartford, CT 06119-2127
U.S.A.

Inquiries: (860) 233-5895
Fax: (860) 233-6072
Order toll free: (800) 289-2664

e-mail: kpbooks@aol.com
Internet: www.kpbooks.com